PALACE PIONEERS

How the first Crystal Palace FC helped create the modern game

Printed in Great Britain and Europe

Softcover ISBN: 9798760017468
Hardcover ISBN: 9798772662892

Imprint: Independently published

Photos: See end of book for full list of credits.
Front cover is how the Crystal Palace players might have looked on cigarette cards of the time.
Back cover is the Crystal Palace cricket ground, a woollen England jersey worn against Scotland in 1872 and the re-made first FA Cup.

Also by the author

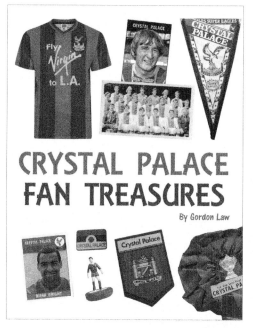

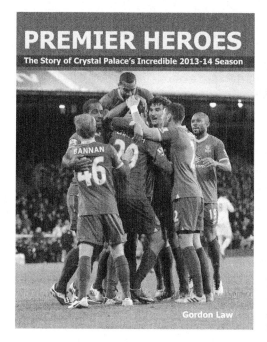

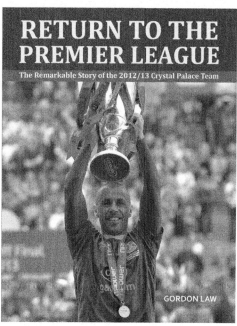

Contents

Introduction

I was always aware of an early Crystal Palace team, apparently formed by workers of the iconic glass building. I became more intrigued when reading further about their fantastic achievements and wrote a short article about these sporting leaders for my Crystal Palace fan site the Holmesdale Online.

It's remarkable to think that a bunch of sports-mad locals, who enjoyed kickabouts in Crystal Palace Park, created one of the first football clubs in the south of England.

After forming in 1861, they went on to organise a unified set of laws for the game with other London start-ups by helping establish the Football Association in 1863. Officials from Crystal Palace FC were among the men who ironed out the rules over the coming years that would conceive modern football.

In 1871, Palace reached the semi-finals of the inaugural FA Cup – the world's first knockout football competition. One of the Palace delegates helped source the original trophy.

Palace players then represented England in the first international fixtures when the English began their annual showdowns against Scotland. They really were a group of trailblazers.

I decided to search the newspaper archives of the 19th Century to discover more about the original CPFC and its personalities. As was common at the time, the side was actually assembled by members of the Crystal Palace Cricket Club and football was a fun outdoor pursuit for gentlemen to keep fit during the winter.

National records reveal the players were educated at the country's leading schools and universities, where they played football under differing rules. These stockbrokers, civil servants and business owners resided in large houses and were wealthy enough to be able to take a weekend or afternoon off to play with their friends or associates.

The Palace men led interesting lives and many of them worked across the globe. Some were associated with the Royal Family, there was a famous actor, while another died on the Lusitania and has a Mexican town named in his honour.

The notion that the team was made up of employees of the Crystal Palace is false. Inaccurate details can spread quickly, especially in the age of the internet. Authentic reports from the 1800s help eliminate the modern-day factual errors and I hope to put these straight in this book. However, if you do notice any errors or can provide further information or images for an updated edition, then please send me an email to: editor@holmesdale.net.

It is vital that historical facts are verified where possible. In Peter Manning's book 'Palace at the Palace: A History of the Crystal Palace and its Football Club 1851-1915', he claims the team appeared in light blue and white colours. I have found no evidence of this.

He also asserts that today's Crystal Palace FC is a continuation of the one born in 1861, which makes it the oldest league club in the world. In my research, I have not identified any link between them. The premise is that the Crystal Palace Company (CPC), which owned the exhibition centre, also controlled the cricket and football clubs. I have found this not to be the case.

Crystal Palace Cricket Club only leased its playing grounds from the CPC and the football team had on-and-off agreements to play on a portion of the field. Reports show the CPC was just the landlord and the clubs were run by their own committees.

When the Crystal Palace football team disbanded in 1876, it relinquished its FA membership and a newspaper article later reported that it "came to grief owing to a misunderstanding with the Palace authorities about their ground."

Then in 1895, the press spoke of a "newly-formed club" that was set up by the CPC. It mostly consisted of players from Corinthian FC and the scratch team played three exhibition matches in three seasons.

There were no more fixtures until 1905 when the media reported of "the new Crystal Palace Club". The CPC was the major shareholder of this "new venture". It's here that Crystal Palace, known as the Glaziers with the new colours of cardinal red and light blue, was founded.

I hope you enjoy reading about the adventures of these eminent Victorian sportsmen. Although the amateur Crystal Palace was a separate entity, I feel it must be recognised in the present-day club's origin story and also its importance to South London.

Without the organised matches at Crystal Palace Park, subsequent FA Cup Finals and England fixtures, the next Crystal Palace FC may never have formed. We owe those Palace pioneers much for helping to invent the beautiful game and their spirit lives on through the team we now call the Eagles.

Gordon Law

The Crystal Palace in Hyde Park for the Grand International Exhibition of 1851

The Crystal Palace now rebuilt and enlarged in 1854 at the top of Penge Peak next to Sydenham Hill

The Crystal Palace

Crystal Palace Football Club has one of the most unique names in the world game.

It comes not from a town or city, but an iconic glass building in South London that is recognised in the team's crest.

The Crystal Palace was first built in Hyde Park, London, to mark the Great Exhibition of the Works of Industry of all Nations in 1851.

Prince Albert and other members of the Royal Society for the Encouragement of Arts, Manufactures and Commerce organised the project as a celebration of modern industrial technology and design.

Architect Joseph Paxton was enlisted to design the huge glass and iron structure to showcase British science and industry and it earned the nickname 'crystal palace' during its construction.

Queen Victoria and Prince Albert officially opened the world's largest building with almost one million square feet of floor space on May 1, 1851 in front of a crowd of more than 25,000.

Travel agent Thomas Cook arranged special trains on the newly-built rail network and many tourists crossed the English Channel by boat from France, Belgium and Holland.

It was a roaring success, with six million people visiting the first-ever 'expo' from that summer to October – averaging more than 40,000 each day – and the profits more than paid back investors.

When the exhibition was dismantled, a group of private individuals saw an opportunity to purchase the building materials and re-house the structure elsewhere.

The Crystal Palace Company (CPC) was formed and planned to raise £500,000 to erect a new palace at the top of Sydenham Hill in Norwood, South London.

Around 350 acres of land was purchased from Leo Schuster and a Mr Lawrie and the company was headed up by Samuel Laing, chairman of the London, Brighton and South Coast Railway Company.

Fellow directors included: civil engineer John Scott Russell, who later built the world's largest steamship; P&O shipping founder Arthur Anderson MP; co-founder of the Midland Bank (now HSBC), Charles Geach MP, with Paxton appointed as director of winter garden, park and conservatory.

The company wanted to create an English Palace of Versailles with magnificent gardens, beautiful flowers and trees from across the globe – and the grandest fountains in the world.

A new railway line would be laid direct from London to the site with a single ticket covering travel and entrance to the park which "will be as thoroughly English in its aspect as the palace itself will in its contents to be a miniature of the world," according to the London Standard.

The work started in 1852 and the new Crystal Palace was completed two years later with a different design and was vastly larger – around twice as high and double the width of its predecessor.

Two tall glass towers at either end housed giant tanks that could hold around 1,600 tonnes of water each – enough to shoot the largest fountains up to 200 feet in the air.

The new Crystal Palace was unveiled by Queen Victoria on June 10, 1854, and 30,000 attendees huddled in the building with a further 70,000 outside to witness the grand opening.

Inside, the Victorians were able to admire Egyptian and Roman art, browse naval

Both Crystal Palaces hosted grand exhibitions of culture and industry

The first dinosaur sculptures in the world were unveiled at the Palace in 1854

artefacts, gaze at stuffed animals, take in various animal shows or watch circus acts. Among the attractions in the 200-acre parkland of colonnades, temples and lakes, were the world's first life-size dinosaur sculptures which are still present today. It became the world's largest building again and the site one of the first theme parks.

Like many large construction projects, costs had spiralled out of control and further capital of £300,000 in shares was raised to complete the grand project. The first year yielded a profit of £12,300 after dividends were paid out and the number of visitors dropped from almost a million over the second half of 1854 to about a third of that for the first six months of 1855.

Queen Victoria visited the park during the building works and she returned the following year to formally open six great fountains, water temples and waterfalls – another example of British engineering feats.

Having the finest waterworks in the world came at a cost and the CPC was always looking for new ways of generating income.

For many years, the company's revenue was affected by closing on Sundays due to trading laws made to encourage worship. This prevented the average working man from visiting parks, museums and concerts on their only day off.

The Ancient Order of the Foresters and its 21,000 members were invited to put on an archery competition in 1856 and the Early Closing Association of workers held a fete with more than 17,000 members.

The CPC built a giant amphitheatre to house a choir and orchestra of around 3,000 people for the inaugural Frederick Handel Festival in June 1857, watched by Queen Victoria and Prince Albert on the final day.

A new cricket ground was created at the bottom of the park for the summer of 1857 under the management of Surrey's Thomas Sherman. Crystal Palace Cricket Club was formed shortly after and paid the CPC a yearly rent for use of the field.

To play for this new amateur side, it would cost an annual subscription of one guinea, along with the park season-ticket price of two guineas.

On August 1, 1857, two cricket matches were played between staff from a London brewery with the Morning Advertiser reporting the first mention of football at the park grounds.

Cricket was the most established sport in the country, with spectators turning out in their thousands to watch the leather-on-willow game. It would be another attraction for the park as football in its modern form was yet to be created.

However, the CPC showed an interest in the fledgling sport, placing an advert in the Morning News on January 23, 1858: "Football – Experienced players will be in attendance on Monday next, to superintend the Game of Football to be played on the cricket ground. Sport to commence at eleven o'clock."

The fountains in full flight in front of the Crystal Palace lower terrace

The beautiful game

The origins of football go back to medieval times, with hundreds of people playing a violent game of chasing the ball 'on foot' in the village streets or fields.

From the 1850s, British public schools and universities began adopting their own contrasting versions of the sport. Some liked a more physical contest, carrying the ball in hand, kicking opponents in the shins and rugby-style scrimmages.

Others preferred running with the ball on the ground without the fear of having a leg or nose broken. Players would rush forward in a group, with one person dribbling and the other taking over. When a defender got hold of the ball at the back, they simply booted it over their heads.

The rules between the different football codes were very different and some students played a variation of both. Winchester College opted for a small pitch of 80x27 yards, Harrow School's area was 100x150 yards and the Sheffield rules stated a maximum size of 100x200 yards.

At Eton, its goals were 11x7ft, Sheffield's size was 8yd x 9ft and the Harrow School width was 12ft with no height limitation.

To score in the Sheffield or Eton games, you had to kick the ball inside the uprights and under the crossbar or tape. While at Rugby School, the ball had to be kicked between the posts and above the 10ft bar. Laws for kick-offs, offside, handling, free-kicks and duration were widely varied.

The institutes, having perfected their rules over many years, would tend to play inter-house matches or annual fixtures against their old boys. Games against other schools took place under the regulations of the home team.

The rivalry between Harrow and Eton and protection of their own games meant they would never face each other, even if there was a common consensus on the rules.

Football clubs later chose a particular set of laws, whether it was the Cambridge University ones that are similar to today's game or the handling variations which were favoured by Rugby School.

Club matches were more akin to Sunday league football, fought on muddy public fields on Battersea Park or Clapham Common with no changing rooms. Before kick-off, sides would have to agree on how long the game should last, the number of players or if tripping and handling should be accepted.

A Victorian-era football match between Old Etonians and Blackburn Rovers

Two umpires would occupy a half each with players having to appeal for decisions such as goals or fouls. If the umpires – represented by each club – were unable to agree, then they 'referred' the decision to an independent official who was situated on the sideline.

Over time, this person would become the 'referee' and the umpires would run the line waving hankies to indicate offside or the ball going out of play as linesmen.

Cricket and horse racing were the most established sports during the 1800s and took up most of the coverage in the newspapers.

Periodicals such as Bell's Life began printing brief football reports supplied by public schools and then the fledgling clubs as fixtures started sprouting up all over the country.

Club reps from the 'ball carrying' and 'ball kicking' factions would write to the newspapers to insist that their code of football was the best.

The game was a mess and needed a unified set of laws. As England entered the 1860s, a bunch of football enthusiasts sought to put that right.

A football team is born

1861/62

It's a new dawn for the sport of football, a big bang moment that will ignite the game in South London and eventually take off across the world.

Crystal Palace Cricket Club established its own football team in the autumn of 1861, probably to keep its players active during the winter months.

Founded in 1857 on the grounds of the Palace, the cricketers leased their field from the Crystal Palace Company and played against local teams such as Sydenham, Dulwich and Stockwell.

Theodore Lloyd, Timothy Bevington, Frank Day and Wickham Noakes were among the batsmen and bowlers to revert to chasing a football.

They played an early form of football that was quite different to today but popular in many of the country's public schools and universities.

With passing not quite established, players would line up in offensive formations and dribble until they were tackled, there was no fixed goalkeeper, typically two defenders and nine forwards.

During this era, leisure time was a privilege for the upper and middle classes who were able to play sport on a Saturday or midweek afternoon in the spirit of pure enjoyment.

Kickabouts between friends on the cricket field was fun, but the new Crystal Palace football club needed a competitive fixture and went in search of an opponent.

There were few organised teams as the game was in its infancy with no common set of rules – but it turned out that East London-based Forest FC were also looking for a challenger.

They had been founded in 1859 by old public school boys from Harrow and Forest School pupils who wanted to continue playing football after they left.

On March 15, 1862, the newly-formed Crystal Palace FC took part in an historic fixture against Forest FC at Leytonstone.

It was a big deal because neither had played a known external match before and it would be based on Cambridge University's football laws.

Brothers Walter and Edward Cutbill were instrumental in organising the match. They had been educated at Forest School in Walthamstow, which had strong links with nearby Forest FC. When the family relocated from Dalston to Sydenham, the siblings played for Crystal Palace.

The teams did not favour the ball-carrying and hacking rugby football rules popular at Blackheath Proprietary School and Richmond.

In a keenly contested, 15-a-side clash Palace were defeated 1-0 by Forest.

Bell's Life in London and Sporting Chronicle was a big weekly sporting paper that mainly covered racing, cricket and boxing. It would publish match reports from the country's elite schools and Palace's first outing made it in print.

"The play on both sides was acknowledged to be very good and that the game was hardly fought is shown by the fact that the only goal won was obtained after an hour and a half's play," the report read.

The Palace line-up included James Turner, Frederick Urwick and three Lloyd brothers, while Forest featured siblings John and Charles Alcock. This is significant as they would all later help establish the Football Association.

Palace team: Allport, Bell, W Cutbill, E Cutbill, Day, Head, Jackson, R Lloyd, Lloyd, Lloyd, Medwin, Phelps, Sharland, Turner, Urwick.

Charles Alcock, who helped create Forest FC after finishing his schooling at Harrow, later said: "It was the first club to work on a definite basis with the distinct object of circulating and popularising the game."

Forest and Crystal Palace are regarded as the first organised football clubs to make

THE FOREST CLUB v THE CRYSTAL PALACE CLUB.
This match came off on Saturday, the 15th inst, on the ground of the former club, at Leytonstone, Essex. Play began at about half-past two, and ended at five p.m. The result was a victory for the Forest Club, who obtained one goal, their opponents having got none. The play on both sides was acknowledged to be very good, and that the game was hardly fought is shown by the fact that the only goal won was obtained after an hour and a half's play. The players were:—The Forest: Messrs J. F. Allcock, C. W. Alcock, H. Bigland, C. Bigland, C. Jackson, G. W. Mackenzie, J. Morgan, J. Pardoe, jun, J. Robertson, C. Tebbut, A. Tebbut, M Savili, J. E. White, and F. Woodward.—Crystal Palace: Messrs Allport, Bell, Cutbill, P. Cutbill, Day, Head, Jackson, R. Lloyd, Lloyd Lloyd, Medwin, Phelps, Sharland, Turner, and Urwick.

Match report from Bell's Life in London and Sporting Chronicle

an impact in the south of England. Three weeks after their first encounter, Palace made three changes for the return match, but they were well beaten 4-0 in their debut home fixture.

Played in wet conditions over two hours, Bell's Life reported: "It was evident that the Forest Club were decidedly superior to their opponents, who admitted they had it all their own way."

Palace team: W Allport, Bevington, W Cutbill, E Cutbill, Day, Jackson, T Lloyd, H Lloyd, A Lloyd, Noakes, Sharland, Turner, Urwick, H Wood, A Wood.

FOOTBALL AT THE CRYSTAL PALACE.
FOREST CLUB v CRYSTAL PALACE.

The return match between these two clubs came off on Saturday week, on the ground of the latter, at the Palace. The weather, which had been fine for the previous two or three days, was again wet, and the ground was not in first-rate condition. Despite drawbacks, however, play commenced at three o'clock, and continued till five. The result was another victory for the Forest Club, for at the conclusion of the game they had obtained four goals, their adversaries none. Three of these were kicked by Mr Pardoe, and the other by Mr C. Bigland. The play on both sides was good, but it was evident that the Forest Club were decidedly superior to their opponents, who admitted that they (the Forest Club) had it all their own way. The players were—Forest Club: Messrs J. F. Alcock, C. W. Alcock, H. Bigland, C. Bigland, A. J. Burness, F.W. Connery, C. D. Jackson, D. J. Morgan, J. Pardoe, J. Robertson, W. J. B. Standidge, C. Tebbut, A. Tebbut, F. W. Woodward, and A. W. Mackenzie.—Crystal Palace: Messrs W. Allport, F. Bevington, W. Cutbill, E. Cutbill, F. Day, T. Jackson, T. Lloyd, H. Lloyd, H. Lloyd jun. W. Noakes, Sharland, J. Turner, T. Urwick, H. Wood, and A. Wood.

Report from Bell's Life in London and Sporting Chronicle

1861/62 Results
Mar 15, 1862, Forest A, 0-1
Apr 5, 1862, Forest H, 0-4

Appearances
2 – Day, Jackson, Sharland, Turner, Urwick.
1 – W Allport, Bell, Bevington, E Cutbill, W Cutbill, Head, R Lloyd, H Lloyd, T Lloyd, Medwin, Noakes, Phelps, H Wood, A Wood, Allport, Lloyd, Cutbill, Cutbill.

Cadets attached to the Metropolitan and Suburban Volunteer Corps gather on the Crystal Palace cricket ground, in September 1861 (The London News)

Bell's Life in London and Sporting Chronicle was a weekly broadsheet published between 1822 and 1886. Best known as a racing paper, it widely covered football as the sport gained popularity

Onwards and upwards

1862/63

The success of Crystal Palace's inaugural football matches saw the club arrange further fixtures.

Two games with Forest FC were organised and the players ventured back to Epping Forest on March 21, 1863.

Palace scored their first recorded goal, but unfortunately the match report was likely supplied to Bell's Life by a Forest official and fails to mention who got it.

Forest's star player Charles Alcock responded with two strikes to give his side a 2-1 victory and his last effort drew praise from the writer.

"The final rush of this gentleman for the last goal was really magnificent and won great applause," said Bell's Life.

The teams had met earlier in the season but there is no record of the result, though the report mentioned that Forest had ended the campaign undefeated.

FOOTBALL.—FOREST CLUB v CRYSTAL PALACE.
The return match between these clubs came off on Saturday, March 21, on the grounds of the Forest Club. Play commenced at half-past three. The first goal was obtained by the Crystal Palace Club, at about five o'clock. The Forest Club were now getting warm into play, and succeeded during the remaining half-hour—it having been arranged that time should be called at half-past five—in obtaining two goals, both of which were kicked by Mr C. Alcock. The final rush of this gentleman for the last goal was really magnificent, and won great applause. The Forest Club closes for the season, on Saturday, the 4th inst. It has been very successful during the present season, having suffered no defeat in any of its matches.

Report from Bell's Life in London and Sporting Chronicle

Forest had played home and away matches against Barnes FC, which was a new club set up in 1862 by London solicitor Ebenezer Morley, who wanted to give its rowing team a winter pursuit. Alcock scored in both 1-0 victories.

This came after the secretary of Forest placed an advert in Bell's Life stating he "will be happy to make arrangements with the secretaries of similar clubs for matches, to be played during the coming season, on the rules of the University of Cambridge."

Meanwhile, No Names Kilburn FC was another new outfit that sprung up in London. It was founded in 1863 by stockbroker Arthur Pember with the unusual moniker, probably based on stock investors who were typically known as 'Names'.

On April 11, 1863, a Palace team led by captain Theodore Lloyd travelled to No Names in a 14-a-side match.

They suffered a 3-0 defeat with captain Pember notching the first two goals, while Barnes FC founder and captain Morley made a guest appearance for the No Names and scored the third.

After the heavy loss, Bell's Life said: "Mr Lloyd, Mr Head, Mr Cutbill and Mr Turner worked hard for the Crystal Palace men."

The No Names side featured a familiar face in Alexander Morten, who was a Crystal Palace cricketer and would go on to play with distinction as a goalkeeper for Palace for many years. Mentioned in the match report was a peculiar rule that had the teams change ends after each goal was scored.

Palace: T Lloyd, G Dry, Cutbill, Cutbill, Barber, Turner, F Allport, Head, W Allport, D Allport, Collins, Grose, Farquhar, Paine.

The 1862/63 season was an important one in the development of football in how we know it being played today.

A match was played on Saturday, April 11, at Kilburn, between the N. N. and Crystal Palace Clubs. The N. N. soon succeeded in running the ball up to their adversaries' goal, where the Palace men made tremendous exertions, but Mr Pember, the captain of the N. N.'s, succeeded in kicking a goal. After a change of goals, Mr G. H. Pember, Mr Groom, Mr Piggott, and Mr Scott made a capital rush, which was successful, Mr G. H. Pember winning the goal. In the third game Mr Morley, backed up by the Bakers, led the way, and after a hard fight succeeded in winning a third goal for the N. N.'s in a manner that elicited a round of cheers. The beautiful play of Mr Giles and Mr Morten was much admired. Mr Lloyd, Mr Head, Mr H. Cutbill, and Mr J. Turner worked hard for the Crystal Palace men. N. N's. A Pember (Capt), E. C. Morley, F. Groom, D. Piggott, G. Lawson, A. Daly, A. Baker, J. Baker, H. W. Baker, W. F. Baker, G. H. Pember, F. Giles, A. Morten, C. Scott.—Crystal Palace: T Lloyd (Capt), G. Dry, H. Cutbill, G. Cutbill, A. G. Barber, J. Turner, F. Allport, H. Head, W. Allport, D. Allport, F. Collins, G. Grose, W. Farquhar, T. Paine.

Report from Bell's Life in London and Sporting Chronicle

A Forest FC team photo, taken in October 1863, with future Palace player Charles Alcock (fifth from left)

Crystal Palace, Forest, Barnes and No Names forged strong connections and they would soon spearhead the formation of the Football Association. Alcock would later describe these clubs as "the backbone of the Association game".

They all favoured the Cambridge University laws of football, drawn up by a group of students in 1848 and nailed to the trees surrounding Parker's Piece common, believed to be the first time that football had any formalised rules.

1862/63 Results
Mar 21, Forest A, 1-2
Apr 11, NN Kilburn A, 0-3
*There was a Palace v Forest fixture but the result is unknown.

Appearances
1 – T Lloyd, Dry, Cutbill, Cutbill, A Barber, Turner, F Allport, Head, W Allport, D Allport, F Collins, Grose, W Farquhar, Paine.

Meeting held 26th October at Freemasons' Tavern

Meeting held 26th October 1863 at Freemasons Tavern

Proposed by Mr Morley
Seconded by Mr Mackenzie
and carried "That Mr Pember do take the Chair".

Propd by Mr Morley
Secd by Mr Steward
and carried "That the Clubs represented at this
The clubs represented at this meeting now form
meeting now form themselves into an
association to be called "The Football
The Football Association
Association"

whereupon the following clubs were
enrolled

Clubs	Represented by
N. N. Kilburn	Arthur Pember
Barnes	Edr C. Morley
W O War Office	Ed. Wawn
Crusaders	H. T. Steward
Forest Leytonstone	J. F. Crook
Perceval House / Blackheath	G. W. Shillingford
Crystal Palace	Frank Day
Blackheath	Fredk H. Moore
Kensington School	W. J. Mackintosh
Surbiton	R. Bell
Blackheath P. School	W. H. Gordon

Propd by Mr McKenzie
Secd by Mr Wawn
and carried "That Mr C. C. Morley be Honorary
Secretary to the Association"

Facsimile of the original 1863 minute book of the Football Association

The FA is established

The public schools and local football clubs were still unable to agree on a standard set of rules when they would play each other and this would lead to bitter disputes.

School members would write to the press stating why their regulations should be adopted by the majority – but they were far from coming to any kind of compromise.

Step forward Ebenezer Morley, the London-based solicitor and founder member of Barnes FC.

Morley placed a notice in the newspapers calling for a meeting at the Freemasons' Tavern, in London, "for the arrangement and adoption of a general code of rules to regulate this healthy and invigorating game so that matches may be fairly contested," published the Sporting Life.

> There is to be a meeting held at the Freemason's Tavern on Monday, by the foot-ball clubs, with a view to framing regular rules and conditions for that noble and popular game. It is expected that the captains of very many clubs will attend.

Bell's Weekly Messenger, October 24, 1863

Crystal Palace, represented by 25-year-old Frank Day, were among the clubs present on October 26, 1863, when the Football Association was born.

Along with Morley, Arthur Pember from No Names Kilburn and John Alcock from Forest FC, were also present. Apart from Charterhouse, it was noted that the major public schools did not attend.

The 11 at the historic first meet were: Crystal Palace; Barnes; Forest; NN Kilburn; War Office; The Crusaders; Blackheath; Perceval House; Charterhouse School; Kensington School and Blackheath Proprietary School.

"Mr Pember (NN Kilburn) was requested to take the chair," read the minutes. "And in doing so said that it had been felt to be desirable to form some set of rules which the metropolitan clubs should adopt among themselves as there were so many different ways of playing, in order that, when they met in a friendly rivalry on other grounds the existing exceeding difficulty of 'getting a goal' would be more easily overcome."

Morley proposed: "That it is advisable that a football association should be formed for the purpose of setting a code of rules for the regulation of the game of football."

Mr AW Mackenzie (Forest, Leytonstone) seconded the resolution.

Pember was appointed president, Morley was nominated the honourable secretary and Francis Campbell of Blackheath was named treasurer.

James Turner, aged 23, was the Crystal Palace rep when clubs met at the Freemasons' Tavern for the second meeting on November 10, 1863.

The nine in attendance were: Barnes; Crystal Palace; Royal Naval School, New Cross; NN Kilburn; Kensington School; Forest; Perceval House, Blackheath; War Office and Blackheath. Four clubs from the initial meeting failed to show up.

Barnes FC founder Ebenezer Morley set up a London meeting to form the Football Association

In a letter read out by Morley, Charterhouse and Harrow said they had declined to join the association, while Westminster sat on the fence.

"At present, Harrow is not willing to join the Football Association," read their letter, as reported in Bell's Life.

"We cling to our present rules, and should be very sorry to alter them in any respect. Therefore we will remain present as lookers-on till we can judge what appears to be done."

After long discussion, the rules of the association were agreed and the first nine laws were thrashed out, from the pitch dimensions to kick-offs and how a goal is scored. However, there was still more work to do and a third session was set up for seven days later.

Thrashing out the laws

The sport was played in multiple combinations of today's rugby and football – but Crystal Palace were among the clubs who wanted the pushing, hacking and handling components kept out.

That was dealt a blow when James Turner was joined at the third meeting by his teammate Henry 'Harry' Lloyd, 22, at the Freemasons' Tavern on November 17.

The attendees were: NN Kilburn; Blackheath Proprietary School; Crystal Palace; Royal Naval School, New Cross; Kingston School; Blackheath; Barnes; Perceval House, Blackheath and the War Office.

Forest FC were absent, so it left Palace and their allies Barnes, NN Kilburn and the War Office out-voted on a series of fundamental 'rugby style' laws given to secretary Ebenezer Morley to refine.

From the nine original draft laws, a total of 23 were now agreed, which included:

12. "A player is entitled to run with the ball in his hands if he makes a fair catch or catches the ball on the first bound."

13. "A player may be hacked on the front of the leg below the knee while running with the ball."

14. "Tripping shall not be allowed except when running with the ball."

15. "A player may be held when running with the ball."

16. "Hands shall not be used against an adversary except when he is running with the ball."

Turner was accompanied by Henry's older brother Theodore Lloyd the following week for meeting four at the Freemasons' Tavern, in London (November 24, 1863).

James Turner was a Crystal Palace delegate at the FA meetings

Both would have likely been wondering what they could do to reverse the additions that had been agreed.

Ten clubs present were: Barnes; Blackheath; NN Kilburn; Forest; Crystal Palace; Kensington School; Perceval House, Blackheath; War Office; Blackheath Proprietary School and Wimbledon School.

Shrewsbury School and Uppingham School wrote in to say they did not want to be a part of the association after seeing a copy of the proposed 'rugby' laws.

FA secretary Morley privately shared that view and devised a plan. He told delegates that before he could draw up the new laws, he wanted to point out that Cambridge University FC had just created a new set of regulations.

Morley said the FA should not proceed any further without considering these laws, which were agreed by gentlemen from six public schools and put into action in a game the week before.

John Alcock was the representative from the Forest Club

Forest's John Alcock backed him up and said: "That the rules of the Cambridge University Football Club, which have been lately published, appear to be the most desirable code of rules for the association to adopt" and proposed the FA should form a new committee to communicate with the university, reported Bell's Life.

As a fellow supporter of the Cambridge laws, Crystal Palace's Turner "would willingly second that resolution".

But Francis Maule Campbell of the Blackheath Club, who favoured the 'rugby rules', proposed the wording be changed from: "The most desirable code of rules for the association to adopt" to being just: "worthy of consideration".

Morley then countered that the laws of Cambridge University should "embrace the true principles of the game with the greatest simplicity".

Morley and Campbell's wording split the room with eight votes each but chairman Pember's casting vote favoured Morley's amendment.

The Freemasons' Tavern, in Great Queen Street, London, was where the Football Association was formed in 1863. The building was demolished in 1909 and is now the Connaught Rooms

NN Kilburn's George Lawson had a rather ambiguous motion carried: "That the committee be empowered not to insist on the clause in the association's proposed rules which allows running with the ball."

This now meant the committee would be entitled to undo the 'rugby rules' that had been agreed at the previous meeting.

Some representatives then said they had misunderstood the meaning of the amendment and didn't vote because they wished to ignore the Cambridge rules altogether.

Pember stated that although they were unable to overturn the previous amendment as it was voted for, the rugby camp had the option of putting forward their own one.

It was proposed "that the committee do insist upon 'hacking' when running with the ball, in their communications with Cambridge" and it was passed by 10 votes to 9.

The meeting was adjourned and ended in a stalemate between the 'hacking' and 'non hacking' factions.

L A W S

OF THE

University Foot Ball Club.

1. This Club shall be called the UNIVERSITY FOOT BALL CLUB.
2. At the commencement of the play, the ball shall be kicked off from the middle of the ground : after every goal there shall be a kick-off in the same way.
3. After a goal, the losing side shall kick off; the sides changing goals, unless a previous arrangement be made to the contrary.
4. The ball is out when it has passed the line of the flag-posts on either side the ground, in which case it shall be thrown in straight. ·
5. The ball is behind when it has passed the goal on either side of it.
6. When the ball is behind it shall be brought forward at the place where it left the ground, not more than ten paces, and kicked off.
7. Goal is when the ball is kicked through the flag-posts and under the string.
8. When a player catches the ball directly from the foot, he may kick it as he can without running with it. In no other case may the ball be touched with the hands, except to stop it.
9. If the ball has passed a player, and has come from the direction of his own goal, he may not touch it till the other side have kicked it, unless there are more than three of the other side before him. No player is allowed to loiter between the ball and the adversaries' goal.
10. In no case is holding a player, pushing with the hands, or tripping up allowed. Any player may prevent another from getting to the ball by any means consistent with the above rule.
11. Every match shall be decided by a majority of goals.

(*Signed,*)

H. SNOW, J. C. HARKNESS,	*Eton.*
J. HALES, E. SMITH,	*Rugby.* ·
G. PERRY, F. G. SYKES,	*University.*
W. H. STONE, W. J. HOPE-EDWARDES,	*Harrow.*
E. L. HORNE, H. M. LUCKOCK,	*Shrewsbury.*

December 9th,

The Cambridge Rules were several formulations of the rules of football made at the University of Cambridge during the 19th century

The laws are agreed

Crystal Palace sent Frederick Urwick and John Louis Siordet to the Freemasons' Tavern for the fifth FA meeting on December 1, 1863.

Clapham-born Siordet was an indigo merchant in the City of London and descended from a well-known Swiss family. He had never played for CPFC but was a member of the Crystal Palace Cricket Club.

With the handling and non-handling camps at loggerheads, could any further progress be made? Palace were joined by delegates of: Blackheath Proprietary School; Forest; Walthamstow; Blackheath; Barnet; Forest School; NN Kilburn and Wimbledon School.

Blackheath's Francis Campbell opened what would turn out to be a fiery meeting by querying John Alcock and James Turner's motion to talk with Cambridge University about their rules and Ebenezer Morley's subsequent amendment.

He claimed that chairman Arthur Pember had counted the votes 'for' but not counted the votes 'against'.

Referring to Pember, as reported by Bell's Life, Campbell said: "On neither of those amendments, did he take the votes against either of them, and as the number present was 19, if the resolution had been put in the proper form the amendment would have been negatived."

Mr Mackenzie of Forest FC replied: "But everybody might not have voted."

Pember was somewhat irked by an accusation of foul play from Campbell. "I really think Mr Campbell that you are in error," he said. "There certainly was something said, and I replied, 'Why did you not vote?'... Do you move that these minutes are not correct?"

Campbell responded: "No, I will not say that, but I want the resolutions of Mr Alcock and Mr Morley to be expunged."

However, Campbell was unable to get this passed as many of his rugby allies were not present and the minutes from the previous meeting were confirmed and signed.

Sheffield FC – formed in 1857 and playing by their own Sheffield rules – spoke of their disapproval of the rugby element to the game in a letter to the association. Secretary William Chesterman wrote: "[Rules] Nos. 9 and 10 I think are directly opposed to football, the latter especially being more like wrestling. I cannot see any science in taking a run kick at a player, at risk of laming him for life."

Alcock was also against rules 9 and 10, which allowed players to run with the ball and to 'charge, hold, trip or hack' a player running with the ball from being written into the laws.

Morley felt that hacking was acceptable for school kids but not adults whose jobs could be affected by serious injuries like a broken leg, adding it would discourage people from playing.

He said: "I feel that, if we carry those two rules, it will be seriously detrimental to the great majority of football clubs.

"I do not say they would not play with us, but is more probable they would not; and Mr Campbell knows well that the Blackheath clubs cannot get any three clubs in London to play with them whose members are for the most part men in business, and whom it is of importance to take care of themselves... and therefore I cordially agree with Mr Alcock.

"If we have 'hacking', no one who has arrived at years of discretion will play at football, and it will be entirely relinquished to schoolboys."

Blackheath's Francis Campbell

But Campbell felt 'hacking' should be part of the game and claimed that it was now less violent than in previous years.

He said: "I have played football ever since I was eight years of age, and certainly approve now of the [Cambridge] laws proposed to be expunged.

"I am much afraid that there are many of the clubs who will not join the association because they fear that our rules will do away with the skill shown in the game at Harrow and Eton and the pluck so necessary in the game as played at Rugby.

"'Hacking' is the true football game and if you look into the Winchester records you will find that in former years men were so wounded that two of them were actually carried off the field, and they allowed two others to occupy their places and finish the game.

"Lately, however, the game had become more civilised than that state of things, which certainly was, to a certain extent, brutal.

"As to not liking 'hacking' as at present carried on, I say they had no business to draw up such a rule at Cambridge, and that it savours far more of the feelings of those who liked their pipes and grog or schnapps more than the manly game of football.

"I think that the reason they object to 'hacking' is because too many of the members of clubs began late in life, and were too old for that spirit of the game which was so fully entered into at the public schools and by the public school men in after life."

FA president Arthur Pember of No Names Kilburn

President Arthur Pember said: "Perhaps you will allow me to say that I took down 'Fifteen' the other day to play a match, and I was the only one that had not been at a public school, and we were all dead against 'hacking'."

Campbell complained that Alcock should not have put forward the Cambridge rules resolution. He added that if the handling and 'hacking' rules are taken out, then Blackheath would withdraw its name from the association and discuss the matter with the other clubs and schools.

Pember reminded Campbell that several other London clubs were invited to attend the meetings and it was also agreed right from the beginning that the rules be put into proper form by Mr Morley.

Campbell, perhaps justifiably, went on to point out that rules 9 and 10 were revoked when some members of the association did not like them.

Knowing he did not have the voting numbers on his side, Campbell sought an adjournment to the meeting, but his amendment was lost by 13 votes to 4. The original motion was carried and both controversial rules were removed. The Crystal Palace votes were vital in getting the rugby parts of the game taken out of the Association football rule book.

"The President observed that though rules 9 and 10 were expunged, it was quite competent for Mr Campbell to bring the matter up at the next annual meeting, by which time it would be seen how the laws worked," added Bell's Life.

After a three-hour meeting, the rules were now confirmed:

9. No player shall run with the ball.

10. Neither tripping nor hacking shall be allowed, and no player shall use his hands to hold or push his adversary.

11. A player shall not be allowed to throw the ball or pass it to another with his hands.

12. No player shall be allowed to take the ball from the ground with his hands under any pretence whatever while it is in play.

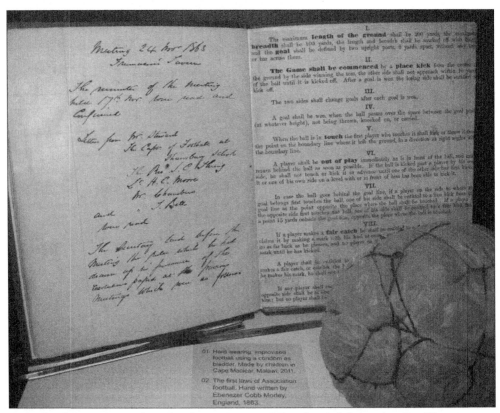

A draft of the original hand-written 'Laws of the Game' drawn up by Ebenezer Morley in 1863 on display at the National Football Museum, Manchester

It's the joy of six

The rules were ratified and an inaugural committee was selected at the FA's sixth meeting on December 8, 1863.

Present at the Freemasons' Tavern were: Barnes; Blackheath; Forest; Crystal Palace; Blackheath Proprietary School; NN Kilburn; Wimbledon School and the War Office.

Palace's Lawrence Desborough and Frederick Urwick were in attendance. Clubmate James Turner was voted on to the FA's committee and is now regarded by the FA as one of its Founding Fathers.

Palace were one of just four clubs to have representatives at each of the six ground-breaking FA meetings where the rules of Association football were shaped. They sent more delegates than any other club and helped keep handling and hacking out of the laws.

Though Francis Campbell was appointed treasurer, he ended the session by saying that Blackheath would be quitting the association in order to continue to play their own code of football.

Publisher and sports retailer John Lillywhite was instructed to publish the FA's official rules, of which half were taken from the Cambridge Rules.

Although the Association football laws were eventually settled with the rugby bits removed, the game of 1863 was still very different to the one we know today. They would evolve over time.

The FA laws allowed a player to stop the ball with any part of the body, including his hands, and also win a free-kick if a player made a 'fair catch' of the ball.

Pitches had no markings, were up to 200 yards long and no crossbar existed on goalposts, so a goal could be scored at any height.

Teams would change ends after every goal, there was no half-time and no set duration, with captains often agreeing to play until it was too dark to continue.

To mark the new regulations, John and Charles Alcock organised a 14-a-side 'test' match in Battersea Park on January 2, 1864 from the FA clubs' best players.

The Sporting Life reported: "The gentlemen who have expended so much time in arranging the new code of laws for the regulation of the game of football had the gratification of seeing them put to practical and highly satisfactory test on Saturday last, when the members of the association mustered in good round numbers at Battersea Park, and played a friendly game, there being fourteen on each side.

"A large muster of spectators, attracted by the fine bracing weather and the novelty of proceedings, attended, and in common with those who took an active part in the game, expressed their entire satisfaction at the working of the new laws."

A Lillywhite's advert for footballs in the Field, 1864

A President's side, featuring Palace duo James Turner and Walter Cutbill, defeated the Secretary's team 2-0, with Palace's Alfred Lloyd on the losing side.

The Albert Tavern pub adjoined the park and was used as changing rooms. The players, members and friends then headed off to the Grosvenor Hotel, in Pimlico, "where a capital dinner and some excellent wines were discussed to the satisfaction of all concerned," added the Sporting Life.

The Prince Albert pub in Battersea – formerly known as the Albert Tavern

Palace kick off new era

1863/64

A piece of history was created by Crystal Palace when they faced off against Barnes in 1864.

The fixture on February 27, was the world's second-ever official football match, played under the Association rules that are universal today.

Ebenezer Morley's Barnes and Arthur Pember's No Names Kilburn had met a month earlier in the first FA-sanctioned game to put the new laws into practice. No Names were 3-0 winners.

Barnes FC, who were founded a year after Palace in 1862, mostly consisted of a team of rowers from the London Rowing Club.

Their club rules stated the home pitch was on Barnes Green, but they moved to play on Barn Elms Park, Barnes, close to the White Hart Inn, where their football equipment was stored.

They were Palace's opponents in this landmark game and CPFC's only documented match of the season. It was due to be played at Palace but was switched to Barnes.

Palace were narrowly defeated 2-1, with the goalkeeping of Palace captain James Turner noted as "admirable throughout the game," reported Bell's Life.

It described one save: "By leaping in the air [Turner] made a catch above his head, in doing which he fell on the goal-post, knocking it down, while he managed very dexterously to roll with the ball on the outside.

"The Crystal Palace were indebted to Mr Turner for services of this character several times during the game."

Palace were the first to score after a long kick by Turner as "Desborough and Sharland ran the ball with great speed behind the Barnes goal, and the latter gentleman, touching it down, made the first goal for the Crystal Palace."

The rules were still some way off the modern-day version as you couldn't pass the ball to a teammate ahead and this report mentions rugby-style rucks and conversions.

Barnes drew level when their player caught a high ball and took it to the ground, making a mark on the pitch, before kicking the ball over the Palace heads between the posts. The FA would spend time over the coming years to eke out these rugby bits of the game to make it what we know and love today.

The Bell's Life report continued: "Each side did their best to win the third goal. The ball, however, showed a preference for the Crystal Palace end of the ground, and after some good play by Greenhill, for Barnes, he kicked the ball through the goal posts.

"But an objection having been raised that one of the Barnes men had just before touched the ball when he was offside, it was allowed, and the ball was again kicked off from the Palace goal line. And in about fifteen minutes Mossenden, for Barnes, succeeding in punting the ball into the adversaries' goal."

There was a return game scheduled for March 26 but no report can be located.

1863/64 Result
Feb 27, Barnes A, 1-2 (Sharland)

Appearances
1 – Turner, Desborough, Sharland, Cutbill.

Goal
1 – Sharland.

Barnes Green (photo mid-1860s) was listed as "the place for play" in the 1862 Rules of Barnes Football Club but they soon moved to Barn Elms Park

The Palace in Penge

1864/65

Crystal Palace kicked off the campaign at a new ground, playing down the road on a pitch behind the Crooked Billet pub in Penge.

Old rivals Forest visited South London on November 19 and came away with a 1-0 win after Charles Alcock's strike.

A month earlier, the Football Association held its Annual General Meeting where the officers were elected. James Turner replaced Francis Campbell as treasurer after Blackheath withdrew from the FA and Walter Cutbill was picked for the committee.

The laws were "on the whole satisfactory, although several clubs expressed a lingering fondness for some favourite rule of their own, which they had to abandon for the sake of promoting the grand object of the association – uniformity," said Bell's Life.

Palace returned to action on December 3 in a goalless draw away at Ebenezer Morley's Barnes. Henry Lloyd, R Abraham and L Irons caught the eye for the 'CPC' (Crystal Palace Club) as they were sometimes known.

There was another stalemate a week later when Palace went to NN Kilburn. The 15-man Palace side had two extra but did not make it count. Walter Cutbill and R Abraham stood out, while Turner's "long kicking was very good," wrote Bell's Life.

The game had a rule currently used in American football which allowed the offensive team a free kick at the goal (with no crossbar), just like a conversion, if they made a 'touchdown' behind the opposition's line.

The New Year opened with a 0-0 against newly-formed Clapham Common Club, who were not fully clued up with the FA's rules. Bell's Life wrote: "The CPC soon obtained a touch down, but the place kick was unsuccessful... Owing to the superior weight of the CPC, the ball was more frequently behind the goal of the CCC."

There were no goals again in a 15-a-side return match with Barnes on February 4, at a muddy Penge. "The ground was in a dreadful state, being almost under water, and the grotesque appearance presented by the players towards the end of the game, through constantly rolling in the mud, may be more easily imagined, than described," said Sporting Life.

A rare goal was scored when Palace made the visit to Forest FC at the end of the month, but unfortunately it was the Leytonstone side who nabbed it in a 1-0 success.

After a lacklustre campaign where Palace had failed to score a single reported goal, they ended it in style with two fine victories. The team sealed their first-ever recorded win on March 4, 1865, with a brilliant 2-1 triumph at Barnes.

John Sharland fired Palace in front with "a fine long kick" before the hosts levelled the scores after the hour mark. As both sides searched for the winner, an unnamed Palace player secured the victory.

A large number of people turned out to watch Norbiton host Palace for their first fixture in a 15-a-side game on Oil Mill Lane, in Kingston. Palace found their shooting boots by banging in five in a 5-1 success against the Association football newcomers.

Melhuish's goal for Palace was the only one mentioned in the Surrey Comet's match report. "Seeing now that the Norbiton club got rather a thrashing it is but fair that the extenuating circumstances should be mentioned the same as previous convictions against a prisoner," it read.

"The Crystal Palace cricket and football club has been established three or four years, and its members meet regularly every week for a match or practice. It therefore ranks among the first flight. There were a great number of spectators present in the field and adjoining lane, throughout the play, who seemed highly delighted with the exhibition, novel to most of them."

It seems that up to this point, Palace had no unified set of shirts as the report notes: "The sight of 30 players in many colored costumes was very pretty."

<u>1864/65 Results</u>
Nov 19, Forest H, 0-1
Dec 3, Barnes A, 0-0
Dec 10, NN Kilburn A, 0-0
Jan 7, CCC H, 0-0
Feb 4, Barnes H, 0-0
Feb 25, Forest A, 0-1
Mar 4, Barnes A, 2-1 (Sharland)
Mar 11, Norbiton A, 5-1 (Melhuish)

<u>Appearances</u>
4 – H Lloyd, Turner.
3 – W Cutbill, W Allport, Sharland, Irons, Morris, Rhode, Grose, R Abraham, D Allport, F Collins.
2 – A Cutbill, E Abraham.
1 – F Allport, E Cutbill, Lloyd, Melhuish, Cluff.

<u>Goals</u>
1 – Sharland, Melhuish.

Crystal Palace played matches in a field behind the Crooked Billet in Penge. The pub was rebuilt in 1840 with its history of a coaching inn going back to 1601

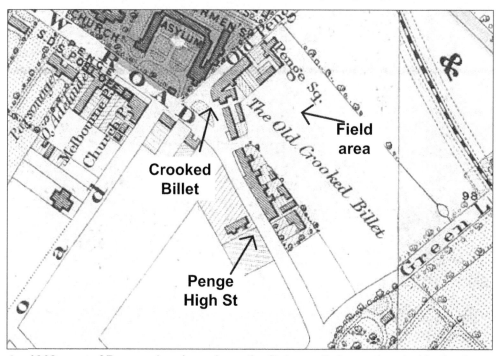

An 1862 map of Penge showing where the Palace pitch was located in the town

Frank Day

Born: 1838
CP career: 1862
Appearances: 2

Frank Day appeared in Crystal Palace's first matches against Forest in 1862, but didn't feature after that. Born in Westerham, he was a player and secretary of Crystal Palace Cricket Club and he took up the same role with the football team.

The Brixton Hill resident represented Palace at the historic inaugural FA meeting in October 1863. With teammate Wickham Noakes, he was co-owner of the Black Eagle Brewery, in Bermondsey, which had many pubs under the trading name of Day, Noakes & Sons.

The Three Tuns, in Beckenham, was one of the Day, Noakes & Sons pubs

Frederick Urwick

Born: 1842
CP career: 1862
Appearances: 2

The Clapham native was in the side for Crystal Palace's initial double fixture against Forest in 1862. The wine merchant was not selected again but he played a major role in forming the unified football laws by acting on behalf of the club at the fifth and final FA meetings in London.

An indifferent season

1865/66

With Crystal Palace now an established football club, they recruited two quality players over the close season.

John Cockerell came into the side and Alexander Morten joined from London rivals No Names Kilburn.

Led by captain James Turner, Palace enjoyed a 2-1 win at home to Clapham, on October 28. Turner and R Abraham were on target with Cockerell and T Rhode impressing for the Palace.

Returning to their Penge home on November 11, Palace entertained new outfit the Wanderers, who were formed out of Forest FC and skippered by Charles Alcock.

Despite having an extra player, Palace had to come from behind to force a hard-fought 1-1 draw thanks to a strike from Rowsell.

"For some time, the ball had a sneaking affection for the Palace goal, but by strenuous efforts and plucky play, the Wanderers were kept at bay for nearly three quarters of an hour," wrote the Sporting Life.

"At last however, fortune smiled on them and in one of their fine rushes the first goal was kicked by JB Martin.

"The Palace, nothing daunted, determined, if possible, to wrest from them their hardly-earned laurels, and at last they were rewarded, and a goal was cleverly kicked by Rowsell."

On a Thursday afternoon of November 23, Palace ventured to Forest School, which would later count ex-England cricket captain Nasser Hussain among its alumni. And they returned to winning ways with a 1-0 success due to E Abraham's goal.

Palace could only muster a goalless draw on a waterlogged Penge pitch to Barnes on December 2, despite having five more men – 14 to their opponents' nine.

It was quite common for teams to arrive at a ground short of players due to transport problems or bad weather, which would mean uneven line-ups, so a player or two might be lent to the other side.

Two days before Christmas, Palace hosted Harrow Chequers, a club founded from former pupils of Harrow School. Palace were a man down and borrowed Mr Stephenson from Harrow, who were "unaccustomed to Association rules". Palace's E Abraham got the scoring underway in this Penge clash and Harrow equalised as "the base was obtained no one knows how, run through, somehow or another, in a 'squash'."

Despite notable performances from Cockerell and Walter Cutbill, Palace then suffered a 3-0 home loss to the Wanderers.

It was a family affair in the 14-a-side match on January 6, with Palace including two Abrahams, two Allports, three Cutbills, plus three Lloyd brothers in their line-up.

On February 3, Palace journeyed across South London to meet Barnes. "But as the rain poured down in torrents for some time previous to the hour fixed for the game, only a few of the Crystal Palace team turned up, and there was consequently no game," reported the Field.

Palace's final fixture of the season against Barnes on March 10 was played with a significant new FA rule. The match ended goalless but Barnes were awarded the victory after beating Palace 2-1 on the American football-style 'touch downs'.

Influential captain Turner ("who is a very fine kicker") was absent, so his deputy Morten stepped in. "The game became hot and fast, and the Palace goal was on two occasions only saved by the splendid goal-keeping of Morten," wrote the Field. "Each party was stimulated to the utmost by their respective friends amongst the numerous bystanders."

1865/66 Results
Oct 28, Clapham H, 2-1 (R Abraham, Turner)
Nov 11, Wanderers H, 1-1 (Rowsell)
Nov 23, Forest School A, 1-0 (E Abraham)
Dec 2, Barnes H, 0-0
Dec 23, Harrow Chequers H, 1-1 (E Abraham)
Jan 6, Wanderers H, 0-3
Mar 10, Barnes A, 0-0* Palace lose 2-1 on touchdowns

Appearances
5 – H Lloyd, E Abraham, Cockerell.
4 – Turner, W Allport, A Cutbill, H Foster, T Lloyd.
3 – R Abraham, W Cutbill, Grose, E Cutbill, Morten.
2 – Rhode, A Lloyd.
1 – D Allport, Sharland, F Allport, Melhuish, Rowsell, Dodson, Lintott, Saward, Hammond, Stephenson, A Tebbutt.

Goals
2 – E Abraham; 1 – Rowsell, R Abraham, Turner.

Anerley Hill with the Crystal Palace water tower being constructed, c1855-56

The Crystal Palace end of Penge High Street, Penge, c1899

Wickham Noakes

Born: October 27, 1840
CP career: 1862
Appearances: 1

Wickham Noakes played just once for Crystal Palace, in their second game against Forest in 1862.

Born in Kennington, he held the purse strings as treasurer of Crystal Palace Cricket Club, where he was also one of the top batsmen. He also enjoyed participating in athletics.

Noakes *(pictured in his older years)* lived in Bermondsey at the family run Black Eagle Brewery and traded as 'Day, Noakes & Sons' with teammate Frank Day. He later resided at Selsdon Park, which after expansion of the mansion and grounds, became the Selsdon Park Hotel.

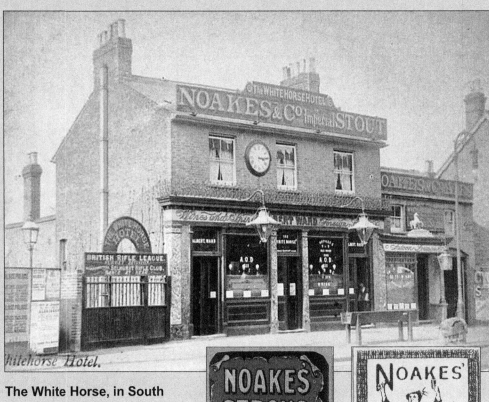

The White Horse, in South Norwood, was one of many Noakes & Co pubs in London

The brewery, which produced its own popular ales and stouts, was sold to Courage in 1930

Major changes made

The Football Association made a giant leap in progress with its rules when members met for the Annual General Meeting at the Freemasons' Tavern.

Ebenezer Morley, who initiated the forming of the FA three years earlier, resigned as secretary due to business reasons.

However, he remained on the committee with Palace's Walter Cutbill, while Charles Alcock of the Wanderers replaced his older brother John. Palace's James Turner was re-elected as treasurer at the February 22, 1866 session.

The FA agreed to adopt an eight foot-high 'crossbar' tape between the posts, so goals would only count if they were scored under it.

Another new rule was that 'touch downs' – where an attacker touched the ball down behind the goal line – would count towards the scoreline if it's a drawn game. Previously, it would give the team a free-kick 15 yards from where the ball crossed the line to shoot between the posts – as in modern-day rugby.

The offside law was amended so a player could now pass the ball forward to a teammate, though you could still be deemed offside in your own half.

Catching the ball with your hands was finally abolished – to bring the FA's laws more in line with the Cambridge ones – but blocking the ball with the hand was OK.

"The Chairman in particular observing that he strongly objected to anything which was not football, as the game had to be played with the feet, and not with the hands," reported Bell's Life.

No Names Kilburn said that few clubs were actually playing by the FA's regulations. "It was also mentioned by the NN representatives that at all times they had found it most difficult to play under Association rules, the Barnes and Crystal Palace clubs being the only clubs they could now play under the rules," added Bell's Life.

"Mr Morley, however, considered that no club in the association ought to play under other rules, and objected to non-members of clubs being permitted to play for a side, in which the meeting generally coincided."

FA members Sheffield FC continued to play by its own Sheffield rules, which was popular among clubs in the city. In March, an 11-a-side London v Sheffield game took place at Battersea Park under Association rules and the southerners won it 2-0.

A man rides a horse and cart on Maple Road, Penge, c1897

Celebrating the coronation of Edward VII at the Penge Recreation Ground, on Penge High Street, c1901

The club is homeless

Crystal Palace were without a home ground when they opened the new season.

After spending two years on a pitch behind the Crooked Billet pub in Penge, the venue was no longer available as it appears new dwellings were built on it. The town was rapidly expanding with residents due to the arrival of the railway.

This resulted in a very brief campaign as the team only played three recorded fixtures, all of which came on the road.

Palace were involved in probably their first 11-a-side match when they lost 2-1 against Reigate on February 9, 1867, on Reigate Recreation Ground.

"The presence of a number of ladies as spectators of the contest enlivened the scene, and added zest to the competition," wrote The Sussex Agricultural Express. It was "a most exciting and evenly contested match" where early on "several [Palace] attacks were repulsed in good style by the Reigate goalkeeper."

An illustration of the Reigate Recreation Ground in The Pictorial World, An Illustrated Weekly Newspaper, 1874

"But at last, after a short run down by W Allport, the ball was captured with rather a lucky kick from another of his side. Reigate then took the higher ground, and their better training (the CPs being short of work this season for want of a ground) began to tell.

"During a scrimmage, in which several prostate players took an active part, the

47

ball was by some means forced between the posts, and a base was secured for Reigate."

Note that rugby-style scrimmages were part of the game at this time and reports continued to refer to a 'goal' as a 'base'.

The report continued: "W Cutbill and the two Lloyds made dangerous rallies for the Palace. Another goal for Reigate was eventually scored by Mr Rowell, who cleverly worked the ball within range, and made a very judicious kick.

"Play was continued with great spirit until time was called but no further goal was obtained, Reigate thus winning by two goals to one. For the CP, W Cutbill (forward) and Cockerell (back) played remarkably well."

Palace returned to Reigate on February 23 and went home happy as Henry Lloyd scored with a "well-directed kick" in the 1-0 win.

After going ahead, "the Sydenhamites had now got thoroughly warmed to their work, and, playing exceedingly well together, managed to keep the ball well in their adversaries' territory, though fortune did not again smile on their efforts," wrote the Sportsman.

Palace's final documented game of the season came on March 9 when they visited Walthamstow to play Forest School. Palace only brought nine players, but were given substitutes and twice went ahead. However, they were held to a 2-2 draw with John Cockerell and old Forester Arthur Cutbill on target.

"For the CPC, Messrs WJ Cutbill, A Cutbill, T Lloyd and S Carver played excellently," wrote the Sportsman.

1866/67 Results
Feb 9, Reigate A, 1-2
Feb 23, Reigate A, 1-0 (H Lloyd)
Mar 9, Forest School A, 2-2 (Cockerell, A Cutbill)

Appearances
3 – Turner, W Cutbill, W Allport, Cockerell, A Lloyd.
2 – A Cutbill, H Lloyd, H Foster, Montresor.
1 – Sharland, E Cutbill, T Lloyd, Morten, R Cutbill, D Allport, Lloyd, Carver, Gardom, Wright.

Goals
1 – H Lloyd, Cockerell, A Cutbill.

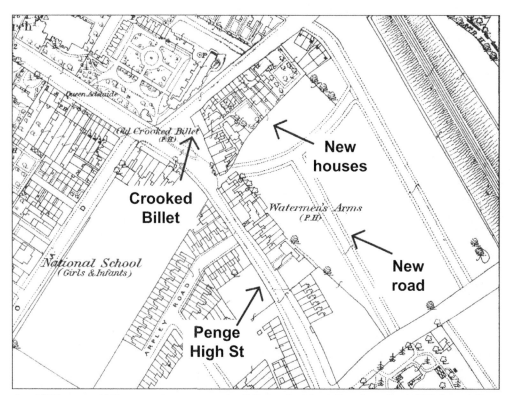

An 1868 map of Penge shows new buildings behind the Crooked Billet and the layout of new roads

Photographed in 2021, a small car park for flats on Green Lane, Penge, takes up some of the area where Crystal Palace's pitch used to be

Beckenham Road, Penge, (now Penge High Street) c1900, with the Crooked Billet located towards the end of this stretch of road on the left

The Victorian three-storey Crooked Billet was damaged during the Second World War with the present-day pub rebuilt in the 1950s

Touch downs no more

Sheffield FC were keen to combine their rules with the FA's so that northern clubs could play their southern counterparts without any disputes.

In a letter to the Sporting Life, a Sheffield correspondent wrote: "Sheffield would be prepared to sacrifice a good deal for the sake of obtaining a uniform code of rules."

Their delegate William Chesterman journeyed to London to the FA's AGM on February 26, 1867, with the aim of making some modifications to the laws.

Just four clubs bothered to appear at the Freemasons' Tavern: Sheffield, Barnes, the Wanderers and Crystal Palace, represented by Walter Cutbill.

Ebenezer Morley replaced Arthur Pember as FA president after Pember stood down from the role. Cutbill was re-appointed to the committee but James Turner did not seek re-election as the association's treasurer.

"Mr Morley said he was a little discouraged at the paucity of attendance that evening when he remembered that at the commencement of the association in 1863 they had a crowded room," reported Bell's Life. He added that "they should seriously consider that night whether it were worthwhile to continue the association or dissolve it."

Among the laws discussed, Sheffield wanted the FA to adopt their version of the offside rule and Barnes suggested doing away with it altogether.

Sheffield proposed the inclusion of an extra "rogue" goal, with flags placed either side of the current goal posts. This would be an amendment to the FA's touch down rule agreed the previous year to decide the result if no goals were scored.

Cutbill of Palace proposed a compromise, suggesting the goal posts be widened by an extra two yards to 10, instead of having rogue flags. But this was overruled as it had not been submitted by writing in advance.

The Wanderers' Charles Alcock said his club's proposed amendments "would be the only step to inducing the public schools to join them. He cited several matches in support of his arguments, and his propositions were carried in preference to those of Sheffield," added Bell's Life.

The result was touch downs were now abolished with no rogues implemented. Rule 7 was amended to: "When the ball is kicked behind the goal line it must be kicked off by the side behind whose goal it went within 6 yards from the limit of their goal."

Support for the FA and its Association rules appeared to be dwindling as only five members turned up for a committee meeting on September 30, 1867. Crystal Palace, with their delegate Cutbill, was represented at Morley's law offices, in Temple, London.

The FA felt that in order to expand the game nationally, it would organise a series of county fixtures as the format worked well in cricket.

It set up a Middlesex v Surrey & Kent match on November 2, 1867, at Battersea Park with Palace's Cutbill and John Cockerell appearing for the latter.

Cockerell was hailed in the press for his defensive play in the first county football match, which ended all square at 0-0.

Cutbill was re-elected to the committee at the next annual meeting of the Football Association, at the Freemasons' Tavern on February 26, 1868.

Crystal Palace proposed the subscription of each club be reduced and to not more than 2s 6d or 5s per annum. The chairman remarked that this would cover the FA's costs and the meeting was unanimously in favour.

Palace's next proposal was to increase the number of the committee from four to 20, but this was rejected after a long discussion as it would add to the numbers "without in any way conducing to the welfare of the association," reported the Field.

PRICE SIXPENCE.

FOOTBALL

LONDON: GEORGE ROUTLEDGE & SONS

With the game growing in popularity, G Routledge and Sons published this 60-page Handbook of Football in 1867

Charles Alcock of the Wanderers proposed an increase of six with "names justly celebrated in the football world, the majority of them old public school men of great fame; and he was certain that their election would eventually secure the co-operation of the public schools," added the Field. This proposal was unanimously carried.

However the Sportsman was encouraged about the growth of the game, writing that there were 475 match reports across various newspapers, compared to 250 the season before, and many new clubs had joined the FA.

Palace make new start

1867/68

Crystal Palace had a 'reboot' of the club following a troubled campaign where they played little football.

After two years at Penge, the pitch was no longer available and the Field newspaper revealed the homeless team was close to folding in the previous season.

"This old-established club, which last year appeared likely to become extinct, in consequence of the loss of their ground at Penge, and the seeming impossibility of obtaining another to suit them, has this year made a fresh start," it reported in December 1867.

"They now play upon a part of the Crystal Palace Cricket Ground and have the advantage of the comfortable pavilion for toilette purposes."

However, the only reported match at Crystal Palace was an inter-club fixture between the Palace 'First Eleven' and 'Twenty Two' on November 30, 1867.

"The fact that thirty-three members put in an appearance in spite of the bitter wind and driving rain, speaks well for the spirit of the club," added the Field.

Spectators gather around the Crystal Palace Cricket Ground pavilion to watch a snow-shoe race in August 1867

The first recorded Palace fixture of 1867/68 came at Forest School a week before Christmas. In a 12-a-side match, CPFC were the dominant side but had to settle for a 0-0 draw in Walthamstow.

Bell's Life said: "If a choice could be made between the two we must give the palm to the Palace, for although they certainly had a great advantage in kicking down hill, the Foresters' goal was at times in most serious danger from repeated runs down by the Palace forwards."

Kent and Surrey faced off at the end of January at the West London Running Grounds, Brompton, and the clash ended in a goalless draw. Walter Cutbill, Douglas Allport and AC Chamberlin represented the Kentish men, with John Cockerell and James Turner appearing for Surrey.

Palace were back on the road when they met Reigate on February 1, and ran out 4-0 victors. They had to lend Douglas Allport and TJ Chidley to Reigate to even the numbers at 10-a-side. It was a comfortable win after goals from CJ Huggins (2) and one each from Walter and Arthur Cutbill.

However, they had their first defeat of the campaign against old friends Barnes on February 22, losing a 14-a-side match 1-0.

Palace went back to Barnes a week later without Turner and Walter Cutbill and

Crystal Palace footballers used the cricket ground's "comfortable pavilion for toilette purposes". Built in 1865, it was replaced by a much larger one in 1899

drew 0-0, being a man down in a testing encounter played in heavy rain.

"Owing to the very unfavourable weather only 10 of the CPs showed up, while the home team numbered 11," wrote Bell's Life. "When [the Barnes forwards] attempted the Palace goal, they were unceremoniously sent to grass by the CP backs.

"After playing with varying success for an hour and a half without a goal being obtained, both sides were glad to give up at the call of 'time'."

On March 14, Palace headed to Walthamstow for the return fixture against Forest School. The South Londoners were playing with two men less and were defeated 3-1, with W Allport on target for Palace.

And they failed to avenge the scoreline when Walter Cutbill took a side back to the school seven days later as Palace ended their campaign with a 0-0 draw.

1867/68 Results
Nov 30, CPFC Twenty Two, H, 0-1
Dec 18, Forest School A, 0-0
Feb 1, Reigate A, 4-0 (Huggins 2, W Cutbill, A Cutbill)
Feb 22, Barnes A, 0-1
Feb 29, Barnes A, 0-0
Mar 14, Forest School A, 1-3 (W Allport)
Mar 21, Forest School A, 0-0

Appearances
7 – A Cutbill.
6 – A Lloyd, R Cutbill, D Allport.
5 – H Lloyd, Sharland.
4 – W Cutbill, W Allport, C Huggins.
3 – W Parr, C Farquhar, R Allport, Cockerell, Butterfield, Chamberlin.
2 – Turner, Chidley, Saward, H Daukes, J Kolle.
1 – Ellis, Morten, B Scott.

Goals
2 – Huggins; 1 – W Allport, W Cutbill, A Cutbill.

Lawrence Desborough

Born: December 4, 1844
CP career: 1864
Appearances: 1

Lawrence Desborough was one of the Crystal Palace delegates who helped draft the first set of Association football rules.

Aged 19, he attended the sixth and final FA meeting with his Palace teammate Frederick Urwick in December 1863.

Desborough *(pictured in 1858)* played just one game for the team. However he made quite an impact, setting up the winning goal against Barnes in February 1864. That match was Palace's first under the FA's unified rules and second ever under the new regulations.

Desborough was also a decent cricketer, making many appearances for Crystal Palace Cricket Club.

Born in Beckenham, the accountant emigrated to New Zealand. He became manager of the Equitable Life Assurance Co office in Bombay.

Desborough sadly died in 1892, in Port Said, Egypt, while en route for England, aged 47.

John Sharland

Born: 1845
CP career: 1862-71
Appearances: 25
Goals: 3

John Sharland was just a teenager when he represented Crystal Palace in their historic first match with Forest in 1862.

The Southwark resident went on to score the club's first recorded goal at Barnes, in February 1864.

Against the same opponents a year later, he got another with "a fine long kick" for Palace's first reported victory. Known for long-range efforts, the forward hit a 20-yard strike against West Kent in 1868/69.

Working as a lithographic printer, Sharland was in the Palace line-up for eight seasons. He was accidentally killed by a stray bullet fired from a neighbour's gun in 1877.

Palace home comforts

1868/69

After a four-year absence, Crystal Palace FC organised a full schedule of matches at their cricket ground home in what was their biggest fixture list yet.

Leading them would be new skipper Douglas Allport who took over from James Turner. The team was also left ruing the departure of John Cockerell who joined the newly-formed Brixton as club captain.

Palace wore blue and white jerseys, recorded the 1868 Football Annual, but there's no further detail of the design. It's possible that it was one-inch hoops as that was the most popular style at the time or players may have worn any shirt with those colours.

CPFC got the new campaign off to a disappointing start when they lost a 12-sided match 1-0 at Barnes on October 31.

There were no fireworks when they entertained Mr AJ Heath's Eleven at the Crystal Palace Ground on November 5, losing 1-0.

The Field wrote: "For the Crystal Palace, who would vastly improve their game by playing more matches and developing their back play. R Cutbill, A Lloyd and A Lintoll were energetic throughout; while H Daukes occasionally exhibited flashes of good style."

Palace travelled to Walthamstow's Forest School in mid-November but the game ended in a stalemate.

They returned to Crystal Palace for the visit of the Wanderers on November 28 and were unlucky to be defeated 1-0.

Charles Huggins' strike was ruled out after the ball had been adjudged to have gone out of play following good work from Reginald Cutbill.

"The ball was driven through the Wanderers' posts by CL Huggins, whose success, however, produced no lasting effect, as the claim of the Palace was disallowed, owing to the ball having previously passed behind the goal line," wrote The Field.

"Both sides exhibited great freedom in knocking on, and hands were used freely and indiscriminately on all occasions."

The FA rule only permitted players to block the ball with their hands, before allowing it to drop, but they were mostly ignoring this, according to the newspaper.

Palace's match at Clapham Common Club on December 12, was delayed for half an hour as no ball or goal posts were available, leaving the teams to play with makeshift uprights. When it got underway, this 0-0 draw was regularly interrupted on Clapham Common.

Bell's Life wrote: "During the game this space was invaded from time to time by 40 gentlemen of the Rugby persuasion, who were playing football upon the adjoining strip, by parties of pedestrians generally accompanied by wet Newfoundland dogs, and by an itinerant vendor of chestnuts, who established his bakery in front of the CP goal."

The 'Sydenhamites' finally got some goals on the board with a 3-1 triumph at Reigate on December 19. They arrived with just 11 men and Reigate lent them a player to make it 12 to the Surrey team's 13.

Nevertheless, Palace went two up through Reginald Cutbill and Theodore Lloyd, before the hosts pulled one back.

Lloyd then got another to seal the win, with Bell's Life reporting: "The ball being well 'middled' to him by H Lloyd. Thus the match ended in the victory of the strangers by three goals to one. For the Palace, R Cutbill, A Lloyd, and CC Harvey played well."

Two days into 1869, new forward Charles Eastlake Smith joined up with Palace for their first meeting with the Civil Service. Huggins got a hat-trick and Alfred Lloyd notched the other in Palace's brilliant 4-0 home win.

"It is but fair to mention that the state of the ground was greatly in favour of the home team, who were accustomed to its 'going', and the CS's being three men short had to be accommodated with emergencies," said the Bell's Life report.

On January 6, the CPs were 2-1 winners against AJ Heath's Team at Crystal Palace, avenging their defeat back in November. Samuel Daukes had levelled the scores before Reginald Cutbill grabbed the winner.

It was a fourth win on the bounce when Palace completed the double over Reigate following a 1-0 victory in Surrey on January 9.

The local press remarked on the Palace backs being extra physical with Reigate forward H Richardson. "The amount of 'charging' to which he was subjected, in consequence, must have been rather trying to his digestive organs," it wrote.

Back at the Palace, the team had to settle for a 0-0 draw with Barnes on January 23.

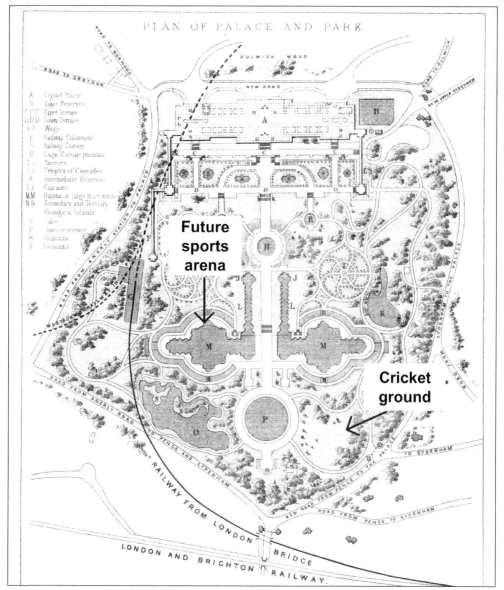

A map of the Crystal Palace Park with the cricket ground located in the bottom right, close to the Penge entrance

"A pitched battle between these ancient clans, whose feud dates back to the dark ages of football was fought at the Crystal Palace," wrote Bell's Life. "A most exciting game followed, neither side appearing to gain any material advantage, but both playing with vigour and energy always characteristic of these meetings."

Morten impressed as a 'rush keeper' as the report continued: "This gentleman, though always in the way when wanted, found time to take a jaunt into the enemy's territory, going express, leaving in his wake a line of prostrate opponents and very nearly achieving a goal for his party."

The old cricket ground in Crystal Palace Park (pictured in 2021) where the Victorian Palace footballers played, facing Crystal Palace Park Road

A physical Barnes team roughed up George Parr who took a while to recover after a heavy fall, while Alfred Lloyd suffered "a severe blow on the nose which destroyed his 'form' and disfigured his feature."

Palace came up against new club Bedouins for the first time on January 30 and gave them a 5-0 thrashing. Bedouins arrived with just six players and borrowed both Kingsford brothers, but were still three players light.

The one-sided nature must have frustrated their captain who was "charging one or two of the smaller growth of the Crystal Palace and depositing them in the mud more than once," wrote a Norwood News correspondent.

"One gentleman who, no doubt, preferred trying the quality of the soil before submitting his clothes to the indignity, went down head first. He found, however, but alas too late, that his head could not preserve the cleanliness of his attire."

Meanwhile, the team travelled to West Kent FC for a February 6 fixture. West Kent was a club that played both Association and rugby rules before it became exclusively a rugby football club.

They lent Palace a player to make it even sides and Huggins got the only goal in Palace's 1-0 win in Chislehurst.

"The goalkeeper of the West Kent team, in stopping a long shot, unfortunately returned the ball against the person of CL Huggins, who was following up, and from the latter it rebounded into the centre of the home goal," wrote the Field.

On February 20, Palace entertained the Clapham Common Club but unfortunately lost by the odd goal. This time, there were no interruptions by stray rugby players or dog walkers on Palace's private ground. Even Cockerell's return for a guest appearance couldn't inspire the lads.

Palace got back to winning ways with a 1-0 success in their first game against Upton Park on February 24. They played matches at West Ham Park, which has no connection to today's professional club. Arthur Cutbill was the CPFC goal scorer.

That week, Palace captain Douglas Allport attended the FA's seventh annual meeting at the Freemasons' Tavern and proposed a rule change.

The Sporting Life reported: "Mr Allport, on behalf of the Crystal Palace Club, proposed that the goal posts should in future be placed at a distance of twelve instead of eight yards apart as at present, but, after an animated discussion, the motion was lost by a large majority."

The proposal by Upton Park to prevent "charging from behind" was unanimously carried. Palace's Walter Cutbill and the other committee members were all re-elected.

Palace held their annual supper at the Clarendon Hotel, Anerley, after an end-of-season club game between the 'Over 23s' and the 'Unders' on February 27, 1869. "Upwards of thirty members and friends sat down, and a most agreeable evening was spent," read a report in the Sportsman.

CC Harvey's 'Unders' lost 4-0 to Morten's 'Overs' and "it is only fair to mention that the juniors would have been much more powerfully represented but for the match Kent v Surrey, which engaged several of their best men," added the newspaper.

Palace ended their season with two away games against old friends Forest FC, who had been reformed since their last fixture in 1865.

Their trip to East London on March 6, which was arranged at 24-hours' notice after Palace's match with the Civil Service had fallen through, resulted in a 2-0 victory.

Palace arrived with only seven players after "only a remnant of the Sydenham team could be tempted down the Great Eastern line," wrote the Sportsman. They were given five boys from Forest School to even the sides.

Theodore Lloyd got the scoring underway, "the ball threading its way with unusual sagacity through a perfect forest of legs" before Forest School pupil T W Crowther nabbed the second.

Palace claimed a 1-0 win in a close game at NN Kilburn on March 13 thanks to Theodore Lloyd's effort. "T Lloyd, by a brilliant dash, secured a goal for the Crystal Palace just as time was called," wrote the Field.

Crystal Palace ventured to Chislehurst Common (before the cricket pavilion was built) where they beat West Kent FC 1-0

CPFC were next on the road to Chislehurst on March 27, where they beat West Kent 2-0, in a match played in slight snow.

John Sharland got the opener when "becoming possessed of [the ball] twenty yards from the West Kent goal, and seeing the latter undefended, took a pot shot thereat, and hit the mark; but the wind is entitled to a commission upon this transaction," reported the Sportsman. Reginald Cutbill "having trundled the ball past all opposition" added another for the Palace.

It appears that goalkeepers were allowed to wipe out opposing players without getting penalised.

The Sportsman added: "[West Kent's] EC Goodhart soon made a good run-up with the ball, and was only stopped and grassed upon the very threshold of the strangers' goal, while the ball went a journey towards Bromley. AC Chamberlin, by this piece of goal keeping, bringing down the applause of the onlookers."

Palace's final game of 1868/69 back at Forest FC on April 10 ended in a goalless draw in Woodford.

"Both sides worked most vigorously, despite the excessive heat of the day, and the play was throughout above average," said the Field's report. "The goal occupied by the Crystal Palace was once or twice in jeopardy, but by dint of the excellent play of A Lloyd, J Sharland and CC Harvey, the visitors succeeded in keeping their lines intact."

Arthur Cutbill

Born: March, 1847
CP Career: 1864-71
Appearances: 35
Goals: 3

Arthur Lockett Cutbill started his footballing life with Forest FC while studying at Forest School, in East London.

The Cutbill family then moved from Dalston to Sydenham and Arthur made his first Palace appearance in 1864.

He became a regular in the back line for many seasons. Arthur was an associate of Lloyds and set up a ship and insurance brokers.

Born in Hackney, he was one of four Cutbill brothers to feature for Palace (Walter, Edward, Reginald).

Timothy Bevington

Born: May 11, 1844
CP career: 1862
Appearances: 1

Timothy Bevington appeared in Crystal Palace's inaugural home game against Forest in 1862, aged 17. He lived in Sydenham and worked as a leather merchant.

Worcester-born Bevington was a Palace cricketer too and later married Annette Currey, the sister of teammate Percivall. His cousin Herbert Shelley Bevington also played for CPFC.

Edward Cutbill

Born: June 16, 1844
CP career: 1862-67
Appearances: 6

One of four Cutbill siblings at the club, along with Reginald, Walter and Arthur. Edward was a teenager when he turned out for Palace's maiden fixtures against Forest in 1862.

Born in Maidstone, he played for Crystal Palace Cricket Club and worked as a London stockbroker, residing in Lawrie Park, near the ground. He was educated at Forest School, in Walthamstow.

63

1868/69 Results
Oct 31, Barnes A, 0-1
Nov 5, Mr AJ Heath's Eleven H, 0-1
Nov 14, Forest School A, 0-0
Nov 28, Wanderers H 0-1
Dec 12, Clapham Common Club A, 0-0
Dec 19, Reigate A, 3-1 (R Cutbill, T Lloyd 2)
Jan 2, Civil Service H, 4-0 (A Lloyd, Huggins 3)
Jan 6, Mr Heath's Team H, 2-1 (S Daukes, R Cutbill)
Jan 9, Reigate A, 1-0
Jan 23, Barnes H, 0-0
Jan 30, Bedouins H, 5-0
Feb 6, West Kent A, 1-0 (Huggins)
Feb 20, Clapham Common Club H, 0-1
Feb 24, Upton Park A, 1-0 (A Cutbill)
Feb 27, Over 23s v Under 23s H, 4-0
Mar 6, Forest A, 2-0 (T Lloyd, Crowther)
Mar 13, NN Kilburn A, 1-0 (T Lloyd)
Mar 27, West Kent, A, 2-0 (Sharland, R Cutbill)
Apr 10, Forest A, 0-0

Appearances
18 – D Allport.
14 – R Cutbill.
12 – A Lloyd, A Cutbill.
11 – Sharland.
9 – Harvey, Morten.
8 – T Lloyd, Chamberlin, C Farquhar.
7 – Huggins, Ellis, WM Allport.
6 – H Daukes.
5 – D Smith, Alpe.
4 – G Parr, C Smith, F Abel, H Lloyd.
3 – Stone, A Lintott, W Parr, R Kingsford, S Daukes.
2 – H Abell, J Kingsford.
1 – Butterfield, Barlow, Trower, Cockerell, Stainburn, Gower, Brown, Crowther, Poole, Walters, Borwick, Mosted, Trinder, H Smith, Jones, G Manvell, R Allport, WH Allport, W Allport.

Goals
4 – Huggins, T Lloyd; 3 – R Cutbill; 1 – Crowther, A Lloyd, Sharland, S Daukes, A Cutbill.

Finally, no more hands

1869/70

When the Football Association convened at its 1870 AGM a significant rule change was agreed – handling the ball under any circumstances shall be prohibited.

"In the event of [it] being strictly enforced, we shall see football carried on as it ought to be, and, as it always has been at one of our principal public schools, made a game of the feet, and free from those unscientific and brutal mauls," said the FA in the Sporting Life.

A sort of half-time was also added to the rules, when "in the event of no goal having fallen to either side at the lapse of half-time, ends shall be changed". Though teams would still switch ends after a goal was scored.

Crystal Palace had no representatives at the meeting on February 23, but Walter Cutbill was re-elected to the FA's committee. Charles Alcock was appointed treasurer and secretary where he would remain for the next 25 years.

Meanwhile, Palace captain Douglas Allport took his side to Forest School in Walthamstow on November 2, 1869, and the match ended 1-1.

The pupils went in front before Palace equalised with "R Cutbill securing this success after a good run down by Lloyd and Stainburn," reported the Field.

On November 26, Palace travelled to meet the Royal Engineers for the first time – a team formed in 1863 and made up of the British Army 'Sappers' based in Chatham, Kent – and lost 1-0.

Influential FA secretary and treasurer Charles Alcock of the Wanderers

The hosts were "frustrated mainly by the excellent back play of CC Harvey, and the good goalkeeping of D Allport, until just before the call of time, when Lieut Dorward brought the ball up into the front of the Crystal Palace posts, and a final kick by Lieut JC Barker accredited the Engineers with a goal," reported the Field.

CRYSTAL PALACE CLUB v. FOREST SCHOOL.
This match will be played at the Crystal Palace to-day (Tuesday). The following will represent the Crystal Palace:—D. Allport (captain), W. H. Allport, A. Borwick, W. Bouch, R. Cutbill, F. M. Hartung, C. C. Harvey, F. Luscombe, G. Parr, and J. Turner.—Train 2.15 p.m. from London-bridge to Sydenham.

The Sportsman, November 30, 1869

Four days later, Palace hosted the return fixture against Forest School and fought out a goalless draw, despite losing two players through injury after 15 minutes.

The team got a win under their belt on December 4 with a 1-0 triumph at John Cockerell's Brixton. They played their matches at the Duke of Edinburgh's cricket ground, in Shepherd's Lane. In the first meeting between the clubs, Theodore Lloyd notched the winning strike.

That same day, a second CPFC outfit led by James Turner drew 1-1 with West Kent at Crystal Palace. Robert Kingsford was on target for Palace.

On December 11, Palace played an internal club game between 'A Morten's Ten' and 'The Rest' (15 players), which finished goalless.

The Ten: Morten (c), H Abell, W Allport, A Cutbill, Daukes, Farquhar, Harvey, J Kingsford, A Lloyd, T Lloyd.

The Rest: D Allport (c), W Allport, Baumann, Capper, Hartung, Lintott, G Manvell, Ormiston, W Parr, G Parr, E Scott, H Scott, J Scott, Stainburn, Traill.

Palace and Barnes went head to head for the first time this season at the ground of the latter a week before Christmas. Like many of these fixtures, the match ended 0-0.

There was another inter-club game organised on December 27 between 'First Half of the Alphabet' and 'Next'.

Heading into 1870 on January 5, Palace were back on home turf when the Wanderers visited Sydenham, but were defeated 1-0.

Palace got back into the winning habit with a 2-0 home success over Mr AJ Heath's Team. "A short and quick run down by D Allport resulted in a goal for the Palace team," reported the Field. "Five minutes from time, CE Smith added a second goal to the score of the Palace team."

That joy was short-lived after they suffered a 1-0 loss at Upton Park on January 26. Palace began the game a player short before Alex Morten later arrived with his side

Gipsies played matches under both rugby and Association codes on Peckham Rye Common (photo c1900) and got changed at the Kings Arms pub opposite

a goal down. "Morten, whose charging had considerable effect in deterring the usually impetuous onslaught of the Uptonians," wrote the Sportsman. RW Abbott went closest to scoring for Palace but the game ended in a defeat.

Palace achieved their first win over the Wanderers with a 2-0 triumph at the Oval on February 9. The CPs having the advantage of 10 players to Wanderers' seven would have made a difference.

James Body

Wanderers thought they had taken the lead when they got the ball through the Palace posts but there was an offside infringement. The hosts eventually fell behind after a defender's clearance cannoned off an unidentified Palace player and crossed the line.

"The change of ends and consequent kick-off was so well followed up by JA Body that another goal was gasetted to the Crystal Palace, the absolute honour of this success being due to a neat kick by F Luscombe," reported the Field.

Norwood-born Luscombe and James Body (with William Parker) had founded a rugby rules football club in 1868 called Gipsies, which was made up of old boys from Tonbridge School.

With Palace's scheduled fixture against West Kent called off, they arranged a game against the Gipsies on their Peckham Rye ground (on March 5). It's possibly the only time Palace ever played under amended rugby laws as set by the home team.

The Sportsman reported: "The rules played were in accordance with those of the home team, with the exception that running with the ball was not allowed unless taken on a fair bound.

"Both clubs came strong as to numbers, the Crystal Palace having seventeen and the Gipsies sixteen men... Almost immediately a goal was put to the credit of his side by a very pretty run and drop by RK Kingsford."

Luscombe equalised for Gipsies as the match ended 1-1, but the Gipsies were handed the victory after scoring the most conversions and touch downs. Gipsies went on to become one of the founder members of the Rugby Football Union, with Luscombe and Body winning caps for England.

Ten men of Palace met an 11 of Brixton on March 12, with Theodore Lloyd scoring in a 1-0 away win. "A speedy rush by T Lloyd, and a slip of the defending back, led to the fall of the Brixton goal," reported the Sportsman.

"The home goal had two or three very narrow escapes, one very hard shot at short range by RL Allport, almost doubling up the Brixton goal-keeper.

"For the CP, Harvey and RL Allport were in excellent form as backs, but the forwards generally played with a great disregard to the necessity of timely middling, and as a result, the ball was taken no less than 23 times behind the Brixton goal line.

"The noticeable exception to this practice was T Lloyd, who always played with his head, and set an example to his juniors."

The recent FA law banning goalies from handling the ball seemed to be ignored by the players. The Sportsman said that: "the new rule of 'no hands' was strictly adhered to throughout, but it was understood that it would not be insisted upon in the case of the goal-keeper. With this modification it appeared to give general satisfaction."

On the same day, Palace sent a team captained by Alfred Lloyd to Woodford to play the Forest Club. The game ended 0-0 and the Sportsman said: "We may add that goals were changed at half-time."

Palace went back to Forest a week later, but they were defeated 2-1. The first half was an even affair before Forest scored two quick-fire goals shortly after the interval. "After this double misfortune the Palace team playing together in better style, succeeded in scoring a goal," wrote the Field.

CPFC faced off with Upton Park on March 26, in the final game of the season and it ended 0-0. The "Palatials" as referred to by the Sportsman started brightly but were indebted to the goalkeeping skills of Morten who repelled the Upton Park attack.

William Parr

Born: January 25, 1844
CP career: 1867-69
Appearances: 8

William Parr was a Crystal Palace cricketer who came into the football side in 1867/68.

The Sydenham resident was secretary of the cricket club and occasionally lined up with brother George in the CPFC team.

Parr *(pictured in his older years)* was born in Gotham, Nottinghamshire, and worked as a solicitor's clerk. He married Helen Lloyd – a sister of the Lloyd brothers.

Reginald Cutbill

Born: June 1849
CP Career: 1867-69
Appearances: 24
Goals: 4

The youngest of the Cutbill brothers, Reginald was another to have made an impact at Crystal Palace Football Club.

Coming into the side at the end of 1866/67, the Sydenham local featured regularly for two years. He worked as a clerk and later became a merchant.

Born in Hackney, his best goal return came in 1868/69 with strikes in Palace victories over Reigate, Mr Heath's Team and West Kent.

Charles Kolle

Born: January 21, 1848
CP career: 1870-73
Appearances: 19
Goals: 2

Charles Kolle wasn't a regular in the Palace team but he had a knack of scoring vital goals when called upon.

His memorable winners came against the Civil Service and Reigate Priory in 1872. Like teammates Walter and Edward Cutbill, he was educated at Forest School, in Walthamstow. Kolle lived in Tulse Hill, earning his living as a clerk.

1869/70 Results
Nov 2, Forest School A, 1-1 (R Cutbill)
Nov 26, Royal Engineers A, 0-1
Nov 30, Forest School H, 0-0
Dec 4, Brixton A, 1-0 (T Lloyd)
Dec 4, West Kent H, 1-1 (R Kingsford)
Dec 11, A Morten's Ten v The Rest, H, 0-0
Dec 18, Barnes, A, 0-0
Jan 5, Wanderers H, 0-1
Jan 11, Mr AJ Heath's Team H, 2-0 (D Allport, C Smith)
Jan 26, Upton Park A, 0-1
Feb 9, Wanderers A, 2-0 (Luscombe)
Feb 12, Barnes H, 0-0
Mar 5, Gipsies A, 1-1* (R Kingsford) Gipsies win with 8 tries
Mar 12, Forest A, 0-0
Mar 12, Brixton A, 1-0 (T Lloyd)
Mar 19, Forest A, 1-2
Mar 26, Upton Park A, 0-0

Appearances
13 – D Allport.
10 – G Parr.
8 – Morten, Harvey.
7 – Turner, R Kingsford, WM Allport, H Abell.
6 – A Lloyd, A Cutbill, Abbott.
5 – Capper, J Kingsford, Hartung.
4 – C Farquhar, T Lloyd.
3 – R Cutbill, Borwick, Luscombe, Stainburn, G Manvell, Ellis, Tovey, C Huggins, H Daukes.
2 – W Bouch, E Scott, Alpe, W Parr, C Smith, H Scott, F Abell.
1 – Slater, R Solly, E Manvell, C Barber, W Collins, De Castro, Saxton, Bickley, Body, Heddle, Mann, Brother, R Allport, Clutton, F Kingsford, W Foster, Soden, Moore, WH Allport.

Goals
2 – T Lloyd, R Kingsford; 1 – Luscombe, R Cutbill, D Allport, C Smith.

International football

The FA needed to expand the game to the whole of Britain so Charles Alcock believed that organising an England team to play Scotland would raise its profile.

Scotland had yet to form its own association, so interested players were invited to apply to FA committee man and Wanderers player Arthur Kinnaird, a Londoner with Scottish ancestry.

Most of the clubs north of the border competed in rugby football, so the Scotland team was made up of players with Scottish heritage who played Association football in England. Their line-up included MPs WH Gladstone and JW Malcolm.

The Sportsman listed Palace's Alfred Lloyd in the England line-up in the morning of the game but he had to drop out due to a prior appointment.

ENGLAND v. SCOTLAND

This International match, according to the rules of the Football Association, will take place at the Oval, Kennington, to-day (Saturday), play commencing at three o'clock. The following players have been selected to represent the two countries:

England: A. H. Thornton (Old Harrovians), A. Baker (N.N.'s), E. E. Bowen (Wanderers), W. P. Crake (Harrow School), E. Freeth (Civil Service), T. C. Hooman (Old Carthusian), A. Lloyd (Crystal Palace Club), F. Lubbock (Old Etonian), A. Nash (Clapham Rovers), J. C. Smith (Crusaders), and R. S. Vidal (Westminster School).

Scotland: J. Kirkpatrick (Civil Service), A. F. Kinnaird (Crusaders), W. A. B. Hamilton (Old Harrovian), C. R. B. Hamilton (Civil Service), W. Lindsay (Old Wykehamist), R. E. Crawford (Harrow School), W. H. Gladstone, M.P. (Old Etonian), J. W. Malcolm, M.P. (Old Etonian), K. Muir-Mackenzie (Old Carthusian), R. N. Ferguson (Old Etonian), and Lord Kilmarnock (Old Harrovian).

The England and Scotland squads named in The Sportsman, March 5, 1870

Alex Morten played as a late replacement as goalkeeper for the Scots, despite being born in Paddington, Middlesex. It was a rearranged fixture after severe frost in London, where parts of the Thames froze over, forced its postponement two weeks earlier.

The world's first international football game took place at the Kennington Oval in London on March 5, 1870, and finished 1-1 after a late England equaliser.

The sides were evenly matched and it remained goalless after 45 minutes when a change of ends was called due to a recent rule if no goals were scored in that period.

Scotland went ahead in the 75th minute after England captain Alcock moved his keeper up front and Robert Crawford of Harrow Chequers found the empty net with a long-range shot.

England got an 89th-minute equaliser when Alfred Baker of the Wanderers went on a fine run through the Scottish defence to fire past Palace goalie Morten.

Morten impressed for the Scots with the Sportsman reporting "only with Morten's determined goal-keeping, that the Northerners succeeded in preventing the English from reducing their goal."

The FA's Arthur Kinnaird (*pictured in 1905*) helped organise the world's first football international

Watched by an estimated 500 supporters, there is no mention of umpires and referees in reports, which suggests that any disputes were settled between the captains.

Critics north of the border challenged the credibility of the Scotland team as none were born in the country – however all would have qualified under today's rules. Many of the Scottish clubs were upset that the first football international was played under the FA's rules and not by their favoured rugby football version.

Queens Park in Glasgow was the only Scottish club to adopt the Association game, though many Scots would have played it in the public schools of England. Nevertheless, the first football match between two countries ended in a draw.

Kinnaird selected and played in the Scotland team. He appeared in a record nine FA Cup finals with the Wanderers and Old Etonians and his landmark of five victories stood until 2010, when it was broken by Ashley Cole.

He was an FA committee man at the age of 21, in 1868, becoming treasurer and then FA president in 1890. Kinnaird would remain in that role for 33 years until his death in 1923, just months before the opening of Wembley Stadium.

Celebrating 10 years

1870/71

Crystal Palace football club entered its 10th anniversary season and celebrated with a win at home to Upton Park.

Charles Chenery made his Palace debut and Charles Eastlake Smith, Frederick Soden and Alfred Borwick got the goals in a 3-1 win.

"The game was maintained in the midst of a heavy rain and under circumstances the ground utterly unfavourable for dribbling purposes," reported Bell's Life.

"So that there was an absence of any great skill on the part of the individuals, and a general lack of energy visible on the part of the visitors, which greatly conduced to their defeat."

Palace played a midweek fixture at Forest School, and without captain Douglas Allport, fell to a 2-1 loss.

The home team took the lead, before Palace's guest star Charles Alcock levelled the scores with "a long side kick". The schoolboys went back in front shortly afterwards.

"Before the conclusion of the game a short run by Alfred Lloyd produced the claim of a second goal for the Crystal Palace, but an objection was raised," reported the Field.

"The visitors were, it is fair to state, a poor sample of the strength of their club, and their chances would have been materially improved with the aid of a little more accuracy of aim."

In Crystal Palace Park, Palace locked horns with Barnes on November 12. "It was arranged that the Association rules should be observed, but the return is to be played under the old regulations," said Bell's Life.

The encounter finished all square and the report continued: "It is now more than two years since a goal has been scored in a match between these clubs, and about three-fourths of their contests from the beginning have been undecided."

Alex Morten was one of the umpires for the second 'unofficial' England-Scotland game at the Oval a week later.

"Messrs A Morten and MP Betts were most assiduous in their positions as umpires, doing everything in their power to ensure a satisfactory termination of the game," wrote the Nottinghamshire Guardian.

Palace's CC Harvey was named in the 28-man England squad by the select committee, but he failed to make the final XI for the match on November 19.

Douglas Allport was among the 11 club captains given the task of picking the team as former Palace man John Cockerell and Alcock helped England triumph 1-0. Robert Walker of Clapham Rovers put away the winning goal.

Morten swapped his umpire's outfit for a Palace shirt for the season's first clash with the Wanderers back at the Oval a few days later. Unfortunately, Palace went down to a 2-0 loss.

Palace put out a weakened side to Forest at Woodford on November 26 and suffered a 1-0 reverse. It was made even worse as Alfred Lloyd was playing for Forest and grabbed the winning goal.

CRYSTAL PALACE CLUB.

On Monday, t e 26th inst., there will be a game at the Crystal Palace, to which members of all clubs playing the strict Association game are invited. Should the respective numbers promise a fair contest the match will be "Crystal Palace Club v. All Comers." Play to commence at two o'clock.

Crystal Palace placed a notice in the Sportsman (December 24, 1870) looking for a friendly Boxing Day match

On December 17, they were lifted by a fine 3-0 win at Cockerell's Brixton, playing with an extra man on a wet and muddy pitch. Another cousin of Douglas Allport – Denison William Allport – featured for Brixton.

Bell's Life reported: "After some excellent runs on the part of Allport, C Kolle and T Lloyd, the latter from a judicious distance, kicked a clever goal. Ends were changed, but luck remained with the Palace team and two more goals were kicked at short intervals by WM Allport.

"Just before time the Palace goal had another very narrow squeak, but no score being made by Brixton before 4:30, the match was decided in favour of the Crystal Palace by the three goals to none.

"The Association Rules were strictly enforced, but no disputes arose, and the game was characterised throughout by the utmost good feeling."

The victory was even sweeter as the Palace were without star men Morten and

French artist Camille Pissarro's painting of the Crystal Palace with families and carriages making their way along the parade in 1871

Chenery who were representing the South in a match against the North at the Kennington Oval that day. The South ran out 1-0 winners.

On a freezing December 21, FA supremo Alcock appeared for Palace when they faced the Clapham Common Club at home.

Alcock marked it with a goal from Alfred Lloyd's assist with five minutes left to give Palace a win their dominance deserved on a snow-lined pitch. "Of [Frederick] Soden's heavy charges it will suffice to say that they were, as usual, crushing," noted Bell's Life.

Amateur players were uncontracted and free to play for whomever they liked, so when Palace visited the Wanderers on January 18, they found Alcock back on the opposing side as captain. He appeared for multiple teams to keep fit and socialise with friends.

The winter snow hampered many of the games in London with Bell's Life reporting: "Owing to the inclement state of the weather during the past month, the lovers of the manly and exhilarating game of football have had a very quiet time; the grounds have been for the most part clothed in the mantle of snow.

"And when the thaw came, the turf has presented such a wet and heavy appearance, that in most instances it has been found perfectly impracticable to play.

Palace had eight players to the Wanderers' seven at the Oval "probably to there being some doubt as to the certainty of the match taking place," added the newspaper.

The Field wrote: "[Palace] worked well at times, but they were deficient in the skill that marked the general play of the victors, and in point of defence were especially weak, owing to the absence of sundry prominent members of their team."

A return match at Upton Park on January 21 saw Palace lose 1-0, "although the visitors left no stone unturned to secure a recovery of their lost ground," wrote the Field.

That same day, Palace put out another team against Hampstead Heathens and it ended 0-0 in Sydenham. "The determination exhibited by the Heathens, who were two short of the regular complement, contrasted with the very feeble play of the opposite forwards," wrote the Field.

At home against Rochester, Palace claimed their best victory yet by thrashing them 6-0. Despite the poor condition of the pitch which made dribbling and running difficult, Frank Alpe gave his side a first-half lead.

The hosts took advantage of their superior fitness levels as Alcock netted twice, then Alpe scored another before Frederick Soden and Theodore Lloyd completed the rout.

The Oval hosted a mid-February showdown between Palace and the Royal Engineers with the fit military men winning 3-1 – played directly after they met Hampstead Heathens.

On February 21, Palace could only muster eight players for their game at Forest School. They were supplemented by three pupils and Theodore Lloyd's goal gave them a 1-0 victory in Walthamstow.

Four days later, England and Scotland drew 1-1 at the Oval, with Walker of Clapham Rovers scoring again. Palace star Chenery was named among the reserves but did not feature.

Palace finished their home campaign with a match between a 'Captain's Ten' and 'Alex Morten's Fifteen'. William Bouch scored "a masterly goal" for Morten's side before Theodore Lloyd levelled matters.

A humorous report in the Sportsman was littered with puns: "The pick of the lot was certainly Robert Allport – there is little change to be got out of such a Bob. Of the Fifteen Morten, as usual, was all there, and if a goal saved is a goal gained, he won the match for his side.

"We were glad to witness the reappearance of Hammond, who, after his three years' rest, came again, like a giant refreshed. Scott, as usual, was good at charging, and the Slaughter was great.

"Who paid the Piper we were not informed, but his services were most valuable.

The Crystal Palace players held their annual supper at the Thicket Hotel on Anerley Road, photo c1893

Finally, we must not omit favourable mention of the marine hairdresser (C Barber) who was never in more clipping form."

Captain's Ten: D Allport (c), R Allport, WM Allport, Chenery, A Cutbill, C Farquhar, Harvey, C Kolle, T Lloyd, C Smith.

A Morten's Fifteen: Morten (c), WH Allport, C Barber, W Bouch, Elborough, Hammond, G Manvell, Melhuish, Ormiston, Piper, E Scott, Slaughter, Stainburn, D Smith, Stevens.

That evening, the players and officials sat down for their annual supper at the Thicket Hotel, on Anerley Road.

The Sportsman adding that it being "an excellent repast; and what with smoke and song, wine and warbling, punch and perorations, the hours slid unobserved away and midnight arriving prematurely, the meeting was adjourned until February 27, 1872."

At the FA's February AGM, the hand-ball law agreed the previous year was finally amended – to allow the goalkeeper "to use his hands for the protection of his goal".

After joining the FA committee from the very start in 1864, Walter Cutbill stepped down and his teammate Douglas Allport was elected as his replacement.

Just a few weeks earlier, 21 rugby football clubs and schools, led by Blackheath and

Richmond met in the Pall Mall restaurant, in London, to form their own organisation. The Advertiser reported it was "for the purpose of considering the question of one universal code of rules for the guidance of those clubs playing to the Rugby style… [and] that the society be called the Rugby Football Union."

The present day game of rugby was officially born. And in March, the first international took place between England and Scotland, at Raeburn Place, Edinburgh in front of 4,000 spectators.

Back in South London on March 4, Palace visited Brixton and the encounter finished 0-0. "Towards the end of the game the Crystal Palace decidedly had the best of it," reported the Sportsman.

"And at one time they thought they had a goal, but as the ball had been handled the claim to it was most courteously waived. On perusal of the names appended it will be seen that Palace had a remarkably hot team, whilst Brixton had rather a ragged lot."

The final fixture of the season against the Royal Engineers, in Chatham, on March 18, also ended without any goals. Morton Peto Betts and Cockerell, who had both played for England against Scotland the previous month, appeared for Palace.

"The Crystal Palace played well together, the doubling of Mr Betts being especially good, whilst the kicking of Cockerell as half-backs well deserves notice," wrote the Field.

Alex Morten was praised for preserving his clean sheet, when an Engineers forward "kicked the ball just in front of the posts, through which it was prevented passing by the goal-keeper following up, and had not Morten got rid of the ball very quickly both himself and the leather would have been forced through the posts," added the newspaper.

The season came to a conclusion with Palace's Charles Morice featuring for a 'World' team that played against the Wanderers. The match finished in a 1-1 draw in front of a large crowd at the Oval.

George Parr

Born: August 23, 1845
CP career: 1868-70
Appearances: 14

George Parr joined Crystal Palace at the start of 1868/69 and spent two seasons with the club.

In a bruising encounter against Barnes in January 1869, Parr was charged by an opponent, "a heavy fall followed and he remained at a discount for some time afterwards," read the match report. He helped the team to a rare victory over the celebrated Wanderers at the Oval a year later.

Educated at Rossall School, Parr appeared for Notts County in 1865 and he also played cricket for Notts Amateurs.

On moving to South London, he became a member of the Crystal Palace Club to play both football and cricket.

Parr enjoyed track and field too, where he competed in sprinting, the high jump, hammer, throwing the cricket ball and was also good at shooting.

When Parr returned to Nottingham, he became a partner in the law firm Parr and Butlin and made further appearances for Notts County FC in his spare time.

Parr was under-Sheriff for the county in 1900. He is the younger brother of Palace teammate William.

William Stainburn

Born: 1844
CP career: 1869-73
Appearances: 15
Goals: 2

Another of the Crystal Palace cricketers, William Stainburn played in the club's football side during the winter months.

Coming into the line-up for the 1968/69 campaign, the South Norwood resident was an important member of the squad.

Stainburn grabbed a notable goal in Palace's 3-2 win over local rivals South Norwood in January 1873. Born in Southwark, he earned his living as a tea trader and acted as promoter for Douglas Allport's testimonial in 1872.

1870/71 Results
Oct 19, Upton Park H, 3-1 (C Smith, Soden, Borwick)
Nov 8, Forest School A, 1-2 (Alcock)
Nov 12, Barnes H, 0-0
Nov 23, Wanderers A, 0-2
Nov 26, Forest A, 0-1
Dec 17, Brixton A, 3-0 (T Lloyd, WM Allport 2)
Dec 21, CCC H, 1-0 (Alcock)
Jan 18, Wanderers A, 0-3
Jan 21, Upton Park A, 0-1
Jan 21, Hampstead Heathens H, 0-0
Feb 8, Rochester H, 6-0 (Alpe 2, Alcock 2, Soden, T Lloyd)
Feb 18, Royal Engineers A, 1-3
Feb 21, Forest School A, 1-0 (T Lloyd)
Feb 25, Captain's Ten v A Morten's Fifteen H, 1-1 (T Lloyd + W Bouch)
Mar 4, Brixton A, 0-0
Mar 18, Royal Engineers A, 0-0

Appearances
14 – D Allport.
8 – WM Allport, Harvey, Chenery, T Spreckley, Soden.
7 – A Lloyd.
6 – C Smith.
5 – Alpe, T Lloyd, Fletcher, C Farquhar, C Barber, Turner.
4 – R Allport, Alcock, Morten.
3 – G Manvell, Morice, C Kolle, Stainburn.
2 – W Cloete, Luscombe, A Bouch, E Scott, Heath, Hutchinson, H Abell.
1 – W Spreckley, Borwick, W Foster, J Kolle, A Cutbill, W Bouch, Huggins,
R Kingsford, Morris, Cockerell, Baker, Ormiston, Leete, Akenhead, Stevens,
H Lintott, Carver, Elmslie, Piper, Ellis, Betts, Hartung, Knight, Cazenove,
Thomson, Morton.

Goals
4 – Alcock; 3 – T Lloyd; 2 – WM Allport, Alpe, Soden; 1 – C Smith, Borwick.

The Crystal Palace kit

So what were the kit colours of Crystal Palace? The first mention of what the players wore was in a March 1865 match report against Norbiton.

In this game, it appears the team was yet to have a standard uniform. "The sight of 30 players in many colored costumes was very pretty," wrote the Surrey Comet.

Early group photos from other clubs showed various styles of tops. It's possible that players supplied their own shirts as long as they were in the established colours.

Charles Alcock's Football Annuals published a club directory with details of team colours. In the 1868 edition, Palace were listed as simply "blue and white." For the next three years, it was: "Blue and white, with blue serge knickerbockers."

Serge is a tough woollen fabric ideal for physical sport. Historicalkits.co.uk analysed Alcock's records and other sources and found that knickerbockers were only available in white or dark/navy blue at this time.

It would have been common for the term "blue" to be used in this context with "dark" considered redundant. It's probably why the England team has maintained its navy shorts from the 1870s to this day.

In the following annuals, the Palace colours are recorded as: "Blue and white jersey, blue serge knickerbockers and dark blue stockings." In Peter Manning's book 'Palace at the Palace: A History of the Crystal Palace and its Football Club 1851-1915', he claims that Palace played in light blue and white. I can find no evidence of this.

The colours, he says, reflect those of the Crystal Palace building; "painted in such a way it almost blended in with the sky". The structure was made of iron and glass.

Yet Crystal Palace Cricket Club's colours were black, red and lavender. London County Cricket Club, which was founded by the Crystal Palace Company, had dark green with yellow and red.

Light blue was rarely used in kits and would have been described explicitly. On the England-Scotland match card of 1873, Palace forward Charles Chenery is listed as wearing 'blue', while another player is identified with 'light blue'.

It's likely CPFC played in blue and white one-inch hoops as that was the most popular jersey design of this era. From 62 shirts of clubs from the south, up until 1876, research by Historical Kits shows 31 of a hooped design, 23 are plain and the remaining eight are a mix of stripes, quarters, halves or a single hoop.

Morton Betts

Born: August 30, 1847
CP career: 1871-72
Appearances: 3

Morton Peto Betts was a leading Victorian sportsman who played a few matches for Crystal Palace.

After attending Harrow School, he represented Harrow Chequers, which was formed by its former pupils.

His first documented Palace appearance came in a goalless draw with the Royal Engineers in March 1871. The previous month, he was in goal for England in an unofficial international with Scotland.

The 1871 Football Annual said Betts was "a neat and effective dribbler, useful in any position."

The 1871/72 campaign was an eventful one for Betts. The Bromley resident featured for Palace against the Royal Engineers, was selected again for England and scored the first-ever FA Cup Final goal.

His strike in the 1872 showpiece won the trophy for the Wanderers. Betts is listed on the team sheet under the pseudonym 'AH Chequer' as the Wanderers had borrowed him from Harrow Chequers.

Born in Bloomsbury, his one official England cap was against Scotland in 1877. The civil engineer also played cricket for Middlesex, Kent and Essex. He married Jane Bouch, a sister of CPFC's William and Alfred.

Robert Allport

Born: 1849
CP career: 1867-74
Appearances: 23
Goals: 2

Robert Allport is one of the family of Allports that played for Palace, often lining up alongside brother Walter or cousins Douglas and William.

His usual position was at the back, "there is little change to be got out of such a Bob," was praise for his performance in one match report.

Allport popped up with some useful goals – a strike in the 3-0 win over Gitanos in 1873/74 and another in the 5-0 triumph over Westminster School the season after. Lambeth-born Allport earned his living as a company accountant.

The FA Cup is launched

The summer of 1871 proved to be another milestone moment in the history of football – the FA Cup was created.

It was the brainchild of FA secretary Charles Alcock, with the concept based on the inter-house knockout competition at Harrow School where he studied.

Four years earlier, Sheffield clubs had taken part in the Youdan Cup which was a knockout contest played under Sheffield rules. Twelve teams took part and Hallam FC won the 1867 final in front of 3,000 spectators.

Back in London at a special meeting at the Sportsman's office on July 20, 1871, Crystal Palace were among the six clubs to agree that a cup competition be organised for the forthcoming season.

"It is desirable that a Challenge Cup should be established in connection with the Association for which all clubs belonging to the Association should be invited to compete," recorded the minutes.

After years of playing friendlies and inter-club games, teams could now compete for a national trophy – and the world's first football cup contest.

FA member clubs were informed about the new resolution and asked to contribute towards the purchase of the trophy. A rule was players could only compete with one team to avoid being cup tied.

When talks continued at a meeting in October at Alcock's Sportsman office, in London, club captains were present to air their views on the matter.

Reported in the Sportsman, Alcock proposed "that a Challenge Cup be given for annual competition, open to all clubs belonging to the Football Association."

Palace skipper Douglas Allport then proposed a sub-committee be set up "to frame a code of rules to be submitted to the approval of a second general meeting" which was agreed.

A week later, the rules were confirmed and the inaugural FA Cup draw was made:

Wanderers v Harrow Chequers
Barnes v Civil Service
Crystal Palace v Hitchin

Donington Grammar School v Queens Park, Glasgow
Royal Engineers v Reigate Priory
Upton Park v Clapham Rovers
Hampstead Heathens (a bye)

Glasgow-based Queens Park were paired with the northern outfit Donington Grammar School to make travel arrangements easier.

Maidenhead and Marlow were added to the draw afterwards but Reigate Priory and Harrow Chequers decided to not take part.

Teams drawn first from the hat did not have home advantage and the clubs had to negotiate the match venue between them.

Palace agreed to play their first competitive game at Hitchin's ground in a field on Bedford Road which is Hitchin Town's pitch today.

The original FA Cup trophy was commissioned by the FA's Douglas Allport of Crystal Palace

Allport and committee members Alfred Stair and Alcock later visited Martin, Hall & Co silversmiths in central London and commissioned the FA Cup trophy.

Standing on an ebony plinth, it had two handles, a figure of a player on the lid and cost around £20 from FA member club donations.

Palace up for the cup

1871/72

Crystal Palace celebrated a decade in existence with a bumper season of fixtures and entrance to the first year of the FA Cup.

Palace warmed up for the new season with Douglas Allport skippering a 'Married' side versus a 'Single' team captained by CC Harvey, watched by "several hundred".

The report in The Sportsman gave some player remarks, describing H Daukes as "youthful and vigorous"; E Field "slow but well proportioned"; A Lloyd as "useful, but not loquacious"; G Manvill "short and broad"; A Morten "prize for best costume"; H Neame "white flannels" and WG Stainburn "benevolent neutrality".

The jovial report continued: "Betts was strong and playful and Bouch was generally agreeable and pleasant. Abell and Smith throughout enlivened the game with the most instructive conversations.

"Of Scott and Farquhar, it can only be said that they charged as little as possible, and that, when compulsion rendered this step necessary, they were evidently bent on inflicting as little damage as possible.

"We have tried to associate Barber with some incident of the game, but have signally failed, and the same remark will apply with equal force to Cloete and Stevens."

Married: D Allport, Alcock, WM Allport, H Daukes, Field, A Lloyd, G Manvell, Morten, Neame, Stainburn.

Single: Harvey, C Farquhar, E Scott, Betts, W Bouch, H Abell, C Smith, C Barber, L Cloete, Stevens.

Palace marked their 10th anniversary with a 1-0 win on October 18 at Clapham Rovers, who were founded in 1869 at the Alexandra Hotel, Clapham Common. With a number of spectators in attendance on the common, Palace opened the scoring in this 12-a-side contest with a goal by Charles Alcock.

The hosts then lost their England international Robert Walker due to injury. Clapham hit the post and fired the rebound over the tape late on before bad light ended matters.

Blue and white-clad Crystal Palace held their first recorded home game of the season on October 21. The drenching rain summed up their performance in a 3-0 drubbing by Royal Engineers when they met in South London.

The Wanderers played their home matches at the Kennington Oval (photo c1860) at a time of no covered stands and fencing surrounded the boundary

Palace made a quick recovery by finally beating Barnes 1-0 at home on November 4.

"Each side drove the ball just over the tape, and once, in addition, A Lloyd only missed the capture of the Barnes goal by a few inches," reported the Field. "The latter goal, however, did ultimately surrender to combined attacks by WM Allport, Clutton and Smith, and, despite all their efforts, the visitors were unable to equalise."

The Palace squad was big enough for Charles Chenery to lead a second team to a 1-0 win at army outfit First Surrey Rifles on the same day. Its football team was started in 1869 and members of the corps played their home fixtures at Flodden Road, Camberwell.

"Soon after kick-off, a goal was obtained by the Crystal Palace by FB Soden, after a good run down by Fleet; an easy chance of a similar success having been previously missed," reported the Field.

Palace put Upton Park to the sword in their first meeting of the season four days later, with Alfred Lloyd on target in a 1-0 home win.

On November 11, Palace travelled to Hitchin, in Hertfordshire, for their historic FA Cup tie and first competitive fixture.

There were few attempts on goal, despite the best efforts of forwards Thomas Spreckley and WC Foster for Palace, who "played well together, and were more conversant with the rules than their opponents," reported the Sportsman.

Palace duo William Bouch and Frederick Soden impressed but it was Hitchin who

Francis Luscombe

Born: November 23, 1849
CP career: 1869-70
Appearances: 5
Goals: 1

Francis Luscombe featured just a handful of times for Crystal Palace. The forward's highlight being a goal scored with a "neat kick" in a victory over the Wanderers.

Luscombe, however, preferred the rugby code and was an integral member in forming its modern game. With fellow Tonbridge School old boys, he founded Gipsies FC which mostly played rugby rules.

The Peckham-based club joined the inaugural Rugby Football Union in 1871, with Luscombe serving on the RFU committee.

Luscombe *(pictured in 1872)* represented England against Scotland in the second-ever rugby international in February 1872, later becoming captain and winning six caps overall.

An insurance broker by profession, he was elected to the role of RFU vice-president and he became a well-known race horse owner. Born in Norwood, Luscombe also competed in athletics and ran for Crystal Palace Athletic Club.

Charlie Harvey

Born: February 4, 1849
CP career: 1868-71
Appearances: 27

Charlie Harvey was a talented back player, earning regular praise for his defensive duties.

The Field reported the Royal Engineers were "frustrated mainly by the excellent back play of CC Harvey" in their game with Palace in November 1869. Harvey was in "excellent form" in defence in a March 1870 win over Brixton.

He was named in the England squad for the second 'unofficial' outing with Scotland in November 1870 but did not make the final XI. Harvey captained an Under-23 Palace side that beat the Over-23s in 1869 and he skippered a 'Single' team against the 'Married' in 1871.

Like his mother, Harvey was a baker and confectioner, based in Godalming High Street.

could have won it near the end. However, they could see no way past the solid half-back John Cockerell and James Turner in goal as the tie finished 0-0.

Both teams made it into the next round under the bizarre Rule 8 of the competition, which states: "In the case of a drawn match the Clubs shall be drawn in the next round or compete again at the direction of the committee."

With Palace through, they made the trek to Godalming, in Surrey, on November 15 for a first outing against public school side Charterhouse.

After the boys got their noses in front, William Bouch levelled matters shortly afterwards. Despite Highton and Spreckley sparkling for Palace, the Carthusians added two further goals to win 3-1.

England and Scotland met at the Oval on November 18, but Alcock did not select any Palace players. Clapham's Walker scored twice in England's 2-1 win.

A few days later, Alfred Lloyd captained a CPFC team that travelled to Forest School in the first of two meetings this season. Forest took the lead and they added another after the Palace goalkeeper slipped on the frosty surface for 2-0.

Charles Alcock went close to pulling a goal back for Palace but his shot flew an inch over the tape. "For the Crystal Palace no one played very well, TF Spreckley and A Lloyd, being perhaps the best," wrote the Sportsman.

Palace were held to a 1-1 draw "in spite of disagreeable weather" when they entertained King's School Rochester on November 23.

The hosts went a goal down but equalised when one of the schoolboys diverted the ball past his own goalkeeper. "No further change took place in the fortunes of the day," wrote the Field.

"It remains to be explained that the Palace played two men short, for J Sharland and AS Thompson left the brunt of the battle and the weather to be borne by their brethren without putting in an appearance."

Alex Morton skippered the Palace team against the Wanderers on November 25, with Douglas Allport unavailable. Wanderers featured the great England cricketer WG Grace, aged 22, on a greasy Oval pitch that was not ideal for dribbling.

Wanderers went ahead but Palace were denied a controversial equaliser, as the Sportsman reports:

A young WG Grace

Walter Cutbill

Born: April 1, 1843
CP career: 1862-68
Appearances: 14
Goals: 1

Walter Cutbill was an integral figure in the Football
Association from the very beginning, serving on the
committee at its first AGM in 1864 up until 1871.

Maidstone-born Cutbill featured in a FA President's v Secretary's game in 1864
which launched the landmark Association football rules. Educated at Forest
School, in Walthamstow, Cutbill was in the Palace line-up for the first games
against Forest in 1862, aged 19.

Residing in Lawrie Park, Sydenham, Cutbill captained Palace over 1867/68 and
won representative honours with Kent and a combined Surrey & Kent team
that season. The forward was with CPFC for seven seasons.

Earning a living as an accountant, he played for Crystal Palace Cricket Club
in the summer. The family company of Cutbill, Son and De Lungo helped build
many railways around the world. His younger brothers Edward, Reginald and
Arthur also turned out for the Palace.

Charles Morice

Born: May 27, 1850
CP career: 1871-75
Appearances: 11

Charles Morice made many guest appearances as a forward for Palace, while
with his main club Barnes. It was here that he was selected for England's first
international against Scotland in November 1872.

Listed as a Palace player, he was picked for a 'World' team that played against
the Wanderers the year before.

His profile in the 1873 Football Annual read: "Has not much weight but is very
fast, and pilots the ball with no little skill and success."

Born in London, Morice caught the football bug while studying at Harrow
School and joined Harrow Chequers after leaving. He worked as a London
Stock Exchange clerk and then became a stockbroker.

Morice was on the FA Committee from 1873-78 and lived in Feltham. He is the
great-grandfather to actors James and Edward Fox, whose nephew Laurence
Fox played DS James Hathaway in the TV drama Lewis.

"Here ensued a discussion creative of great diversity of opinion, those of the Crystal Palace who were near the ball asserting that it had passed the posts, while the three Wanderers who were absolutely in charge of it maintained with equal certainty that it had never crossed the boundary.

"In fault of any conclusive testimony to favour either party the matter was thus left, and soon afterwards time was called."

The Field added: "CE Smith dribbled with great skill more than once and the three (Palace) backs all did their share of the work in a most commendable style."

Palace made full use of their squad by selecting another team that day to face near neighbours South Norwood and – with three extra players – triumphed 3-0.

South Norwood were formed at the beginning of 1871/72, with their home ground listed as a well-maintained field opposite the Spread Eagle pub, on Portland Road.

Meanwhile, Alcock selected Chenery, Percy Currey and Soden in a London side to play a first-ever match with Sheffield on December 2. Known for his tact and diplomacy, Alcock helped maintain the FA's existence by working amicably with the administrators of the Sheffield Football Association.

One of the Crystal Palace towers visible on Westow Hill, Upper Norwood, c1890s

The Londoners returned south nursing a 3-1 loss played under Sheffield rules, in front of more than 2,000 gathered at Bramall Lane.

Maidenhead were drawn by the FA Challenge Cup Committee as Palace's next opponents and the teams agreed to play at Crystal Palace on December 16.

On a damp afternoon, there were few spectators present with the majority coming from Berkshire to cheer on their team for this second-round tie. Palace keeper Morten was late and didn't arrive until just before half-time with Maidenhead having the better of the opening exchanges.

On a heavy, thawed pitch, Alfred Lloyd then put Palace in front, before William Bouch doubled the lead with a shot that went in off the tape and the keeper's hands.

As the light began to fade, Chenery, "who had worked hard and unselfishly throughout", nabbed the third goal to seal victory and a place in the quarter-finals.

The Sportsman put Maidenhead's defeat down to a combination of their "long flannel trousers" and the Palace ground being around half the size of their opponents'".

Giving an insight into tactics of the era, it added: "We noticed a tendency to advance in a bunch instead of in line, which error no doubt partly excuses another – that of continued dribbling when a judicious change by a cross kick would be the true game."

Due to bad weather, Reigate only had six players when they met Palace on December 20. CPFC let them have captain Douglas Allport, Charles Cumberlege and Piper to make it a nine-a-side contest, played in strong winds and blinding rain. Alfred Lloyd and Chenery scored in the second half to give Palace a 2-0 home win.

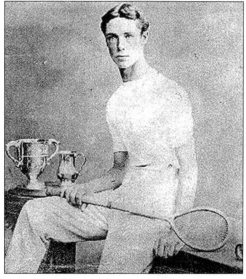

There was no festive cheer for an under-strengthened Palace, when they visited Upton Park two days before Christmas. On a foggy day which deterred some players and onlookers from showing up, Palace were defeated 1-0.

"Morten, emerging from the retirement of his position between the posts, tried to turn the tide of battle by several rapid flank movements, nothing resulted from the efforts," wrote the Sportsman.

Oxford University's Cuthbert Ottaway guested for Palace in the FA Cup

On Boxing Day, Douglas Allport's charges lost 1-0 at home to Harrow Chequers on a waterlogged Crystal Palace pitch.

The Field wrote: "By mutual consent of the captains the play only lasted an hour. Under the most favourable circumstances the space devoted to football at the Crystal Palace is not calculated to favour play, but after heavy rain the ground is in every way adverse to locomotion, from the adhesive nature of its soil and the slippery condition of its surface."

Palace drafted in several new players for their FA Cup third-round tie against the Wanderers on January 20, 1872, played on Clapham Common.

They borrowed Cuthbert Ottaway from Oxford University FC, who is regarded as the most outstanding sportsman of his generation and later became England's first official football captain. His Oxford teammate Frederick Chappell also joined.

The Wanderers marked a sustained period of pressure with Alcock (back at his main club) firing over the game's best chance. The tie ended goalless, though the hosts had a goal disallowed for handball after the break and Palace's clean sheet "was only preserved by the excellent defence of its keeper [Morten]," said Bell's Life.

Winter time at the Crystal Palace parade, Upper Norwood, c1900

James Turner

Born: December 6, 1839
CP career: 1862-73
Appearances: 43
Goals: 1

James Turner is known as one of the founding fathers of football.

He attended the second, third and fourth meetings of the newly-formed FA at the Freemasons' Tavern to help create football's first official rule book.

It is likely Turner, 23, only missed the first meeting as his eldest son had been born just two days earlier. The Croydon native "willingly seconded that resolution" for the FA to adopt the Cambridge football rules which formed the basis of the FA's laws.

Turner was elected to the first FA committee in December 1863 and he became the first 'proper' FA treasurer after Francis Campbell stood down, holding the position from 1864 to 1867.

A Crystal Palace Cricket Club batsman and committee member, he helped establish the Palace football team and played in the opening game against Forest in 1862, becoming captain a year later.

In Palace's only recorded result of 1863/64, the goalkeeper put in an outstanding performance in a defeat to Barnes, with Bell's Life reporting that "Palace were indebted to Mr Turner for services of this character several times during the game."

When the FA organised a match in Battersea Park to demonstrate the new unified football regulations in 1864, Croydon-born Turner was picked for a President's team that beat a Secretary's outfit 2-0.

Turner, whose "long kicking was very good", won a call-up for Surrey in their encounter with Kent in January 1868. He was in goal for Palace's first-ever FA Cup tie against Hitchin in 1871, keeping a clean sheet in the 0-0 draw.

A wine merchant by profession, he was also a committee member and runner with Crystal Palace Athletic Club.

Educated at Streatham Academy, Turner married Rachel Lloyd, the sister of teammates Theodore, Henry and Alfred.

His father Thomas Turner was the first president of the Royal College of Veterinary Surgeons. Thomas Turner Path, linking George Street and Park Street in Croydon, is named in his honour.

93

"The Crystal Palace team worked well together forward, Chappell, Ottaway and Chenery all showing untiring energy."

Chenery and Morten were selected to represent London in the return match against Sheffield, played under FA rules at the Oval on January 27. The Londoners triumphed 1-0 but were bemused by their opponents heading the ball, which was a new concept at the time.

"The use of their hands being entirely forbidden, the visitors resorted to an ingenious method of 'heading' the ball, ie stopping it with the head so placed as to make the ball rebound in the direction it came from," wrote the Yorkshire Post and Leeds Intelligencer.

The Sheffield Independent praised Palace star Chenery, "who will be remembered for his capital play in Sheffield in the last match, baffled his opponents in a truly surprising manner."

On the same day and without the services of Palace's two London players, CPFC were defeated 1-0 at Charterhouse School.

The Penge entrance to Crystal Palace Park on Thicket Road, c1895

John Cockerell

Born: November 22, 1845
CP career: 1865-72
Appearances: 16
Goals: 1

John Cockerell joined Crystal Palace for the 1865/66 season and quickly became one of its star players, earning rave reviews in the press.

The half back was selected for Surrey & Kent against Middlesex for the first ever county football match in 1867. He was praised for his solid defensive play and clean sheet in the 0-0 draw.

The following year, he won representative honours with Surrey. The Camberwell-born back quit Palace to captain new club Brixton in 1868. It was here that Cockerell, 24, was selected for the second and third 'unofficial' England-Scotland internationals in 1870 and 1871.

He returned to Palace for occasional appearances, which included the club's first-ever FA Cup tie against Hitchin in 1871. "Has great speed and knows when to kick, a good dribbler," read his profile in that year's Football Annual.

Cockerell ran for Crystal Palace and South Norwood Athletic Clubs, serving on the latter's committee. He once beat the great WG Grace in a quarter-mile race and also appeared for Crystal Palace Cricket Club.

The Lambeth resident worked as a clerk in his uncle's coal business, which was the official supplier to Queen Victoria and Edward VII.

Charles Huggins

Born: March 28, 1848
CP career: 1867-71
Appearances: 15
Goals: 6

Charles Lang Huggins came to Palace for the 1867/68 season and quickly established himself into the team.

The forward's two goals helped Palace to a 4-0 win away to Reigate in February 1868.

Norwood-born Huggins *(pictured in 1912)* also bagged a hat-trick in a 4-0 triumph at home to the Civil Service in January 1869. A few weeks later, the London stockbroker notched the winner against West Kent to end an impressive campaign with four goals in seven outings.

The 1872 team of Royal Engineers who Palace met in the FA Cup

Palace played their return game at Barnes on February 3, and triumphed 2-0. They had to play with 10 men against the oarsmen after Soden was absent, but they took the lead in the second half through Alfred Lloyd.

"Within five minutes of their first success a well-sustained bully on the Barnes goal line resulted finally in a second goal for the Crystal Palace, the ultimate kick being attributed to WM Allport," reported the Field.

That afternoon, Palace defeated Scoonites 3-0, in Norwood, with Theodore Lloyd, William Stainburn and Robert Smith on target.

At the FA Committee meeting on February 7, it was decided that both Palace and Wanderers should be placed into the semi-final draw after their tie ended all square.

Palace had mixed fortunes when they put out two sides on February 10. Away at South Norwood they were not at full strength and were defeated 1-0.

Hosting the return match against Clapham Rovers, goals from Alfred Lloyd and Chenery sealed a 3-0 triumph for a stronger CPFC line-up.

Palace were paired with Royal Engineers in the FA Cup semi-final on February 17, 1872, at the Oval.

The Sappers had Henry Renny-Tailyour in their side who remains the only person to

Charles Alcock

Born: December 2, 1842
CP career: 1870-73
Appearances: 11
Goals: 5

Charles Alcock is arguably the biggest driving force in developing the game of football.

As a brilliant player and administrator, Alcock's vision took the sport from the parks and public schools to the world stage.

Born in Sunderland, Alcock moved to Chingford, Essex with his family while in his teens. He got into the game while studying at Harrow School and helped set up Forest FC with his brother John to continue playing after they left. Forest became Crystal Palace's first opponents when the teams met in March 1862.

Forest and Palace were among the clubs that formed the Football Association, eventually thrashing out a unified code of rules in 1863.

A sports journalist by profession, Alcock was an editor at the Sportsman and the Field. He launched the first football annual in 1868 – published each year until 1906 – while also penning many other sporting books and periodicals.

As the FA's honorary secretary, it was his idea to introduce the knockout FA Cup competition in 1871. Alcock then organised the first football international by setting up an England team to face Scotland in 1870 and featured in the early matches.

He promoted playing football in a 'scientific' way, advocating passing between teammates instead of individual dribbling. The 1872 Football Annual noted he had "a good shot in the neighbourhood of goal."

The talented forward mainly appeared for the Wanderers – which he founded after leaving Forest – and as captain led them to win the very first FA Cup Final in 1872. He refereed the 1875 and 1879 FA Cup Finals.

Football-mad Alcock relocated to West Dulwich and turned out for Palace in his spare time. He scored in wins over the Clapham Common Club and Rochester in 1870/71, finishing the term as Palace's top scorer.

At Palace's 1872 end-of-season supper, he was dubbed the 'King of Football' and asked to give a tribute to the long-serving Douglas Allport.

Alcock influenced cricket too, playing for the Gentlemen of Essex and the MCC and serving as secretary of Surrey for 35 years. He coordinated the first Test match in England when Australia visited the Oval in 1880.

play for England at both football and rugby. Boosted by Chappell and Ottaway back in the cup team, Palace had to soak up pressure for much of the first half but grew more into it after the break.

"The ball during the first half of the game was kept in the Crystal Palace territory, but was only prevented from being driven between the goal-posts by the greatest exertions on the part of the Crystal Palace back players, indeed on one occasion it was so close that the ball just went over the tape," reported Bell's Life.

"Some good runs by Chenery and Ottaway were much applauded by the spectators. The REs' back players had now some work to do, but their goal was never in any real danger." But again, another of Palace's cup ties finished without any goals scored.

On Tuesday, February 20, Palace took 13 men to Forest School for a fixture against the students. The school had 11 players and asked that two of the Palace team be taken out to make it even.

CPFC had the better of the chances and ran out 1-0 winners thanks to a second-half strike from Kolle.

In-form Chenery, 22, was called up for the first time to the England side to face Scotland at the Oval on February 24. Chappell was named in the squad as a Palace player but was not picked.

Morten had also been selected but ended up acting as umpire for this fifth 'unofficial' international which England won 1-0. Both players had previously appeared for Scotland. Chenery's performance was described as "indefatigable".

Palace completed their home campaign with an internal game between a 'Captain's Eleven' and a 'Rest of the Club' side featuring 23 players, with the latter winning 2-1.

Allport was re-elected to the committee when the FA met for its AGM that week on February 28, at the Arundel Hotel, in Arundel Street, London. Some of the rule amendments made are still active in the modern game.

Clubs must now only change ends at half-time; the ball is still in play if it rebounds off a goal or 'boundary' post and a goal kick is awarded six yards out when the ball is shot over the bar.

As the FA looked to bridge the divide between the football codes, its London team faced Sheffield for the third and deciding match on March 2.

Palace's Morten joined Allport, Soden, and Alfred Lloyd in the London XI, with Chenery and Currey listed as Wanderers players.

Frederick Chappell

Born: July 22, 1849
CP career: 1872-75
Appearances: 5
Goals: 1

Frederick Chappell was one of the Oxford University players Crystal Palace acquired for their first FA Cup foray in 1871/72.

Chappell was a key player in the university's football side after he left Marlborough Royal Free Grammar School. Despite being born in Westminster, he was selected for Scotland's 'unofficial' match with England in February 1871 and was listed under the pseudonym 'F Maclean'.

With Palace competing in the inaugural FA Cup, Chappell appeared in the 1872 ties against the Wanderers and Royal Engineers, but couldn't help Palace from getting knocked out by the latter in a replay.

In November 1872, the Oxford player was selected for England's first 'proper' international against Scotland.

The barrister changed his name to Frederick Brunning Maddison in February 1873 and scored under the new moniker on his Palace return two years later. "A very powerful forward, and one that knows not fear. Is always to be found in the vicinity of the leather," said the 1873 Football Annual.

The front man was an FA Cup runner-up with Oxford University in 1873, then won it in 1874 and again with the Wanderers in 1876. He competed in athletics, rowing, boxing and played tennis at Wimbledon in 1880.

He is the grandson of Samuel Chappell, the founder of Chappell & Co piano manufacturer and music publisher, known today as Warner Chappell Music.

Charles Armitage

CP career: 1871-75
Appearances: 33
Goals: 1

Charles Armitage holds the club record for the most FA Cup appearances, only missing two of Palace's 12 matches in the competition.

The Sydenham native scored against Oxford University in the cup in 1872 but it was in vain as Palace were eliminated by the eventual runners-up. The forward represented Surrey in 1875 and he also competed for Palace in athletics.

In front of 5,000 fans, the first hour was played under Sheffield rules and Chenery deflected a shot home after a fine run by Alcock to put the capital side in front. The northerners soon equalised, and despite the second period being played under London rules, they grabbed the winner for a 2-1 victory.

"[Sheffield] Having an advantage in both sets of rules, stamping unquestionably their superiority over the metropolitan Eleven," reported Bell's Life. "After the match the players and friends adjourned to Mr Arunfield's and partook of dinner... The speeches all tended towards an amalgamation of rules."

With their best players representing London, Palace sent out a weakened side to play the Civil Service that day. James Turner made a rare appearance and captained Palace to a 2-1 win after goals from Theodore Lloyd and Charles Kolle, at the Oval.

The Oval would have seemed like a home ground for many of the Palace players as they returned to the cricket venue for their FA Cup replay with Royal Engineers seven days later.

Chappell was again 'loaned' from Oxford University, but it was a blow that the impressive Ottaway was unable to make it.

The 1872 Charterhouse School first team, pictured in front of the Cloisters, which was where the old Charterhouse football game was played

Robert Lloyd

Born: March 14, 1836
CP career: 1862
Appearances: 1

Robert Lloyd was in Palace's first line-up against Forest in March 1862. He may have been the unidentified Lloyd brother who played in the return game a month later.

Bewdley-born Lloyd married Mary, the sister of teammate Alfred Borwick. The stock broker sadly died in 1873, aged 37.

William Allport

Born: 1836
CP career: 1868-73
Appearances: 42
Goals: 6

William Manning Allport is among the leading Crystal Palace appearance makers.

A cousin of Douglas, Robert and Walter Allport, he scored two goals in a 3-0 win at Brixton in December 1870. William also helped Palace to their first FA Cup victory – a 3-0 success over Maidenhead in 1871.

He impressed in Palace's match with Reigate Priory in December 1872, with Bell's Life writing: "WM Allport took his wing with great avidity, and showed promise of future excellence."

This may have been laced with sarcasm from the club secretary who supplied the report as William was aged 36 at the time. Born in Brixton, he resided in Lambeth and worked for Rothschild bank as an accountant.

Walter Spreckley

Born: April, 1852
CP career: 1870-74
Appearances: 12
Goals: 1

Walter Spreckley played infrequent games for Palace during his four-year association with the club. He got Palace's 1872/73 season off to a flyer by scoring the winner in a 1-0 success over his old school Forest. Born in Notting Hill, he became a wool merchant. Brother Thomas also represented CPFC.

After an evenly-contested opening, a much-fitter Engineers exerted their authority on the tie before they fired in three goals to claim a comfortable victory.

Palace's Morten didn't have the protection goalies have today, with Bell's Life reporting: "The goal-keeper again got mauled, and the post where the melee took place swayed about in the most astonishing fashion, and it certainly looked as if the fragile erection would come to grief.

"For the Palace Chenery was, perhaps, the most prominent, but the greatest praise is due to Morten, the duties of goalkeeper in this match being the most onerous."

Palace's cup adventure came to a sad end as Royal Engineers reached the first-ever FA Cup Final, though the Sappers would go on to lose 1-0 against the Wanderers.

CPFC put out two sides on March 16 and were victorious in both. Alfred Lloyd's strike was enough to give them a 1-0 win at Reigate Priory. "The excellent stand made by Chenery and Morten, on the part of the visitors, prevented the goal of the Palace from falling," reported the Sportsman.

A second-string side captained by William Bouch made the short journey to South Norwood and they ran out 1-0 victors. Palace were bolstered with brothers James and Robert Smith who switched teams for the game.

"The presence of a goodly number of ladies incited both teams to exert themselves, to pass ungraceful tumbles unnoticed, and when they were hacked to try and look as though they liked it," wrote the Norwood News.

James Smith

Four days later, Palace finished 1871/72 on a high with a 2-0 triumph against First Surrey Rifles. John Vigne's double proved the difference between the sides, in Camberwell.

1871/72 Results
Oct 18, Clapham Rovers, A, 1-0 (Alcock)
Oct 21, Royal Engineers, H, 0-3
Nov 4, Barnes, H, 1-0 (WM Allport)
Nov 4, First Surrey Rifles, A, 1-0 (Soden)
Nov 8, Upton Park, H, 1-0 (A Lloyd)
Nov 15, Charterhouse School, A, 1-3 (W Bouch)
Nov 21, Forest School, A, 0-2
Nov 23, Kings School Rochester, H, 1-1 (Own goal)
Nov 25, Wanderers, A, 0-1
Nov 25, South Norwood, A, 3-0 (Own goal)
Dec 20, Reigate, H, 2-0 (A Lloyd, Chenery)

Thomas Spreckley

Born: September 1850
CP career: 1870-74
Appearances: 19

Thomas Spreckley joined Palace at the start of 1870/71 and was a regular fixture throughout the campaign.

The forward *(pictured in 1910)* appeared in Palace's maiden FA Cup fixture against Hitchin in 1871, helping the team get to the semi-final stage.

Born in Marylebone, his younger brother Walter also appeared for Palace and the Essex-based siblings occasionally lined up together in matches. After leaving CPFC, Spreckley continued playing in the FA Cup with new clubs Woodford Wells and Upton Park. He was also a keen cricketer.

The 1877 Football Annual said Spreckley was "very fast down a side; dribbles well, and middles unselfishly; slightly wanting in weight."

His sister Mary married Palace teammate Alfred Lloyd. Earning a living as a warehouseman, his father Thomas senior founded a large textiles manufacturers and wholesalers named Spreckley, White and Lewis.

Alfred Borwick

Born: June 17, 1836
CP career: 1869-73
Appearances: 9
Goals: 1

Alfred Borwick made sporadic appearances for Palace over a four-year spell.

The Walthamstow resident operated at back, half-back and as a forward. Born in West Bromwich, his best moment in a Palace shirt was scoring in a 3-1 win against Upton Park at the start of 1870/71.

Borwick, who worked as an insurance agent and underwriter with Lloyd's, also turned out many times for the Wanderers.

His family created Borwick's baking powder, with George Borwick & Sons Ltd set up by his father. It became the most popular baking powder in the world and is still used by many home bakers today. His sister Mary married Palace clubmate Robert Lloyd.

Dec 23, Upton Park, A, 0-1
Dec 26, Harrow Chequers, H, 0-1
Jan 27, Charterhouse School A, 0-1
Feb 3, Barnes, A, 2-0 (A Lloyd, WM Allport)
Feb 3, Scoonites, A, 3-0 (T Lloyd, Stainburn, R Smith)
Feb 10, South Norwood A, 0-1
Feb 10, Clapham Rovers H, 3-0 (A Lloyd, Chenery)
Feb 20, Forest School, A, 1-0 (Kolle)
Feb 24, Captain's Eleven v Rest of the Club, H, 1-2
Mar 2, Civil Service, A, 2-1 (T Lloyd, C Kolle)
Mar 16, South Norwood, A, 1-0
Mar 16, Reigate Priory A, 1-0 (A Lloyd)
Mar 20, First Surrey Rifles, A, 2-0 (Vigne 2)

FA Cup
Nov 11, Hitchin, A, 0-0
Dec 16, Maidenhead, H, 3-0 (A Lloyd, W Bouch, Chenery)
Jan 20, Wanderers, A, 0-0
Feb 17, Royal Engineers, A, 0-0
Mar 9, Royal Engineers (replay), A, 0-3

Appearances
17 – D Allport.
16 – A Lloyd.
13 – W Bouch, Morten.
11 – Chenery.
10 – WM Allport, Armitage, Fleet.
9 – C Barber, C Smith.
8 – Heath.
7 – A Bouch, E Scott, Soden.
6 – T Spreckley, L Neame, Currey, C Kolle.
5 – Turner, G Manvell, C Farquhar.
4 – H Abell, Alcock, W Foster, Vigne, R Smith.
3 – Chappell, Rouquette, Fletcher, T Lloyd, Stainburn, J Kingsford, H Daukes.
2 – J Smith, E Manvell, Ottaway, Cockerell, Kolle, Piper, Saward, H Lintott, Horne, Highton, Harvey.
1 – Morice, Jack, Weston, Clutton, Frost, L Mann, Rawlinson, W Cloete, Fry, Sharland, R Allport, D Spreckley, Stevens, W Thompson, Sparham, Anderson, Champneys, Slaughter, A Thompson, WH Allport, Burrows, Betts, W Spreckley.

Goals
6 – A Lloyd; 3 – Chenery; 2 – Vigne, W Bouch, WM Allport, T Lloyd, Own goal;
1 – Alcock, C Kolle, Soden, Kolle, Stainburn, R Smith.

Allport gets honoured

Crystal Palace captain Douglas Allport was recognised for his services to the club at the 1872 end-of-season dinner. The details of the occasion from the Norwood News & Crystal Palace Chronicle is reprinted below:

"In the evening the annual Club Supper took place at the Clarendon Hotel, Anerley, about forty members sitting down to a substantial repast, very well put on the table by the new proprietor, Mr Sampson.

"The Chairman (Walter Franks, Esq), after the usual loyal toasts had been proposed, said it was now his most pleasant duty to propose the toast of the evening, which was the health of Douglas Allport, Esq, who, as they knew, had been Secretary, Treasurer, and Captain of the Club for many years.

"And they had only to look at the position of the Club now held as one of the first of the Metropolitan Clubs, and engaged in the last ties for the Association Cup, to know how efficient his services had been.

"They not only valued Mr Allport as one of the best back players and most zealous captains a Club ever had, but admired his character, and appreciated his invariable good sense and good humour.

The Crystal Palace squad held their end-of-season supper at the Clarendon Hotel, on Anerley Road. It was bombed and destroyed during World War Two

"He would now read a paper to which were attached upwards of sixty names, which was in effect that the members desired Mr Allport's acceptance of a testimonial in recognition of his many services and sound generalship as captain.

"The testimonial consisted of a very handsome epergne [table centrepiece] in gilt and oxidised silver, with feur tazzas to match, and an elegant drawing room clock in blue marble and ormolu.

"Mr Allport, in responding, thanked the members very heartily, commenting at some length on the beauty and value of the articles.

"He disclaimed much of the credit which had been given him, saying that the many victories of the Club had been gained chiefly by the way in which the Palace team had always played together, and, to use the technical expression, 'backed up'.

"He felt their generosity the more, as he had probably had more enjoyment out of the Club than any other player; and considered himself more than repaid for what work he did by the honour and pleasure it was to be the captain of such gentlemen and good players as members of the Crystal Palace Football Club (great cheering).

"The Chairman then proposed 'Success to Football' and called on the Captain of the Wanderers, whom he designated the 'King of Football' to respond.

"Mr CW Alcock, who was much cheered, replied. The health of 'The Ladies' of Mr WG Stainburn, the promoter of the testimonial, of Mr A Morten, the Deputy-captain, and of the Chairman having been drunk, and a variety of capital songs sung, the party broke up at half-past 11 o'clock."

Playing Rules of Football by Charles Alcock, US edition 1871

Samuel Daukes

Born: 1845
CP career: 1869
Appearances: 3
Goals: 1

Samuel Daukes joined Crystal Palace in 1869 and the Beckenham resident quickly made his mark.

Born in Cheltenham, Daukes scored in Palace's 2-1 victory over Mr Heath's Team on his debut in January.

A Bell's Life reporter hailed his fine performance against Barnes, stating: "Daukes deserves a doxology" – which is a short Christian hymn of praises to God.

The former Uppingham student was a clergyman at St Bartholomew's Church, in Sydenham, and later became the vicar at Holy Trinity, in Beckenham.

His father Samuel Whitfield Daukes was a highly regarded architect whose list of works include churches and grand houses across England. His younger brother Henry also represented Palace.

Henry Lloyd

Born: July 24, 1841
CP career: 1862-69
Appearances: 22
Goals: 1

With brothers Theodore and Alfred, Henry Lloyd was involved with the Crystal Palace team from its inception in 1862.

Aged 20, Henry appeared in those initial matches against Forest. He then contributed to Palace's first reported win, when they beat Barnes in 1865.

The Thornton Heath resident assisted his teammate James Turner at the third FA meeting in November 1863, helping the new association formulate the first set of football rules.

Camberwell-born Lloyd scored the winning goal in a 1-0 victory at Reigate in 1867 with a "well-directed kick".

He worked as a clerk in shipping insurance and died at sea in 1869, aged 27. He is the great-great grandson of Sampson Lloyd II, who co-founded Lloyds Bank.

Lawrence Cloete

Born: 1850
CP career: 1871-73
Appearances: 6

Lawrence Woodbine Cloete, along with Alexander, Henry and William, was one of four Cloete brothers who represented Crystal Palace FC.

They were the grandchildren of Henry Cloete, who was the British High Commissioner for the colony of Natal – the present-day KwaZulu-Natal, in South Africa.

Their great-grandfather Hendrik Cloete had owned Groot Constantia, which is the oldest wine estate in South Africa.

Its dessert wine is mentioned in the works of Charles Dickens and Jane Austen. While in exile, Napoleon had 30 bottles shipped to St Helena every month.

Playing at the back, South Africa-born Cloete joined Palace in 1871 and made just a handful of appearances during his time with the club.

As a bachelor, he was selected for the Crystal Palace 'Single' team that took on the 'Married' in an inter-club game to kick off the new 1871/72 season.

Also a Palace cricketer, Cloete spent some time as consul in Persia, with the Hampshire Chronicle reporting in 1889 his name on the invitations to a state ball at Buckingham Palace with the British Royal family in honour of his Majesty the Shah of Persia.

Operating as a stockbroker in London, in 1891 Cloete "was charged with obtaining £1,600 from Mrs Annie Page by alleged false pretences," reported the Yorkshire Evening Post. Equal to around £130,000 today.

He and a business associate "were convicted of being concerned together in uttering a certain bogus transfer for shares in the Simmer and Jack Gold Mining Company, with an intent to defraud," reported the Globe at the Old Bailey in 1892.

"His lordship, in the case of Cloete said that he took into consideration the social penalty he would have to pay as the result of this conviction.

"And also the fact that he (the learned judge) believed that he (Cloete) had taken up the transfer of shares under the belief that he would have had the money to pay before he was called upon. He sentenced Cloete to six months' hard labour."

Morten leads England

England and Scotland had already clashed five times before, but the meeting in November 1872 is regarded as the first official fixture between the nations – and the first international football match.

The FA's Charles Alcock was keen to address criticism from north of the border that the Scotland team in their previous encounters were not truly Scottish.

Alcock asked FA members Queens Park of Glasgow to organise trials and recruit a squad of Scotland-born players to play in a new outing against the English.

Taking place at the West of Scotland Cricket Ground, in Partick, on November 30, a crowd of around 2,500 paid a shilling each to watch.

Palace's Charles Chenery, 22, was selected for an England side that was captained by his old teammate Cuthbert Ottaway. Other former Palace players in the line-up included: Frederick Chappell, Charles Morice and John Brockbank.

Having previously played in goal for Scotland, Alex Morten was selected for England in this 'proper' international but he had to withdraw due to illness.

England's woollen jersey for their first-ever international

The Scotland XI was made up entirely of players from Queens Park. It included brothers Robert and James Smith, who briefly appeared for Palace during the 1871/72 campaign.

A strong England forward line led by Ottaway and Chenery both "displaying splendid dribbling" was unable to breach the Scottish defence. England twice hit the post in the second half through Chenery and Arnold Kirke-Smith and the historic match ended 0-0.

Chenery kept his place in the English side for the second 'proper' international against Scotland at the Oval on March 8, 1873 – as did

England had caps and the Scots wore cowls in November's game

half back Robert Smith for the Scots. Having missed the first game, Morten was picked as the English goalkeeper and captain. Aged 41, he still remains the oldest player to make an England debut and is the country's second-oldest international.

Though England and Scotland wore their respective white and blue jerseys, the players were identified by their different coloured headwear and socks. On the match card, Morten is listed as wearing a black cap and brown stockings, while Chenery has a blue and black cap, blue knickerbockers, blue stockings.

Twenty-three-year-old Chenery marked a fine performance by "naturally and patriotically accepting" England's fourth goal in a 4-2 win. There was further Palace representation with Theodore Lloyd, 38, officiating as the referee.

Days later, seven FA-affiliated clubs from north of the border formed their own Scottish Football Association to help drive the popularity of the sport in a country dominated by rugby.

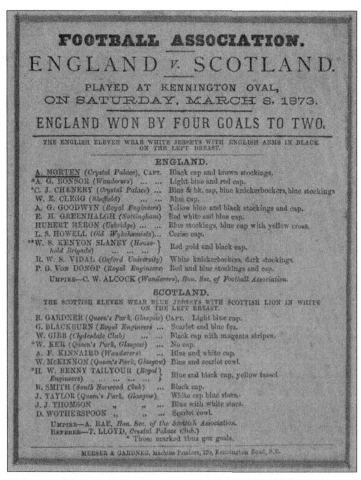

The match card for England v Scotland in 1873 is believed to be the oldest existing football programme

Palace stars sparkle

1872/73

Crystal Palace began the new season with dreams of FA Cup glory after falling one game short of the final the previous year.

Their first-round opponents were Oxford University and the teams met at the Oval, on October 26, 1872. This time Cuthbert Ottaway and Frederick Chappell were in the Oxford line-up, with Ottaway skippering his side.

Palace keeper Alex Morten deputised for the absent Douglas Allport as captain. Starting with a player less, they found themselves three goals down before they even created a chance against arguably the best side in the country.

They managed to peg it back to 3-2 after the break, with goals from Charles Armitage and Lloyd, but Palace fell at the first hurdle to the season's eventual finalists.

Two weeks earlier, Palace made the short journey to Portland Road to face South Norwood and were 2-1 victors. George Fleet capitalised on some early pressure by putting Palace ahead off Laurence Neame's assist.

South Norwood equalised after a change of ends. "Soon after that one of the visitors obtained another goal for his side, which was allowed although the man was called 'off side', and was consequently unmolested at the proper time by the backs," reported the Norwood News.

Charles Chenery and Morten returned to the London side for another 'best of three' against Sheffield at Bramall Lane on November 2. However, despite going in front, the capital outfit lost 4-1 in front of a crowd of around 4-5,000.

Three days later, Palace entertained Forest School. The team was boosted by the additions of Morton Peto Betts, John Brockbank and Charles Morice and they ended up 1-0 victors through Walter Spreckley's strike.

"[Douglas] Allport, who made his first appearance this season, officiating as captain, was in excellent form," remarked Bell's Life.

However, Palace crash landed the following game with a 4-1 reverse against the Royal Engineers.

They then played out a familiar goalless draw away to Barnes in a 10-a-side fixture on November 16.

Despite the likes of Chenery, Morten and Theodore Lloyd returning for the home clash with Upton Park on November 23, Palace lost 1-0.

After the Uptonians took the lead, Bell's Life said: "Responding to the call of their captain (Allport), the Palace now played all they knew to score, and Chenery and Cumberlege were particularly active in the vicinity of the Upton goal.

"On more than one occasion, incautious handling on the part of the visitors enabled the Palace to claim the privilege of a free-kick at critical moments, but luck was against the attempts, and no advantage ensued."

Meanwhile over on Hackney Downs, Alfred Bouch led another CPFC team against Clapton Pilgrims who were defeated 1-0.

On the following Tuesday, Palace played out a 0-0 draw away at Forest School. Palace started with just eight men, so the Foresters lent them some players to even things out but neither could score.

A week after Chenery's appearance for England against Scotland (mentioned in the previous chapter), he was among the scorers in Palace's 3-0 win at home to Reigate Priory on December 7.

"The presence of a body of spectators too numerous to mention by name gave additional interest to the engagement," said Bell's Life. Charles Kolle and Charles Cumberlege notched the other goals, "each being secured after some lively 'in-fighting'."

The report went on: "WM Allport took his wing with great avidity, and showed promise of future excellence. Horne played with energy, and, being fitted with improved extra flexible joints (unaffected by any kind of weather), was valuable in positions of extraordinary difficulty. Mr Soden middled the ball with judgment, and conducted the conversation with his usual urbanity."

Days later, Chenery captained a Surrey side – which featured his Palace teammates Frederick Soden, Alfred Lloyd, Alfred Heath, and Cumberlege – against Middlesex, who selected Morten in goal. Chenery and Lloyd scored in the 4-2 Surrey win as Morten was noted to have "kept goal admirably but was woefully unsupported".

With six players absent, it was no surprise to see an under-strength Palace lose a seven-a-side match 1-0 at First Surrey Rifles, the same afternoon in Camberwell.

A week before Christmas, a depleted Palace lost a goal-laden match 5-2 against the Wanderers, at the Oval. Palace's Robert Kingsford took advantage of some slack home defending to cancel out an early strike from the Wanderers.

However, the hosts scored three quick goals to move into a 4-1 lead. Kingsford

John Vigne

Born: 1854
CP career: 1871-75
Appearances: 31
Goals: 2

John Vigne ended his first campaign in style by scoring
a double in Crystal Palace's final-day 2-0 win over First
Surrey Rifles in 1872.

The Bromley resident was chosen in a Candidates XI for a trial match for
England's game with Scotland in 1873.

However the Notting Hill-born half back, who was a stockbroker by profession,
missed out on the final squad.

Percivall Currey

Born: March 28, 1851
CP career: 1871-74
Appearances: 18

Percy Currey marked an impressive first season at Palace by getting selected
for London against Sheffield in 1871. Earning a living as an architect, Currey
was a regular in defence for the following three years.

Educated at Eton, he lived in Penge Lane and continued to play for the Palace
cricket team into his 40s.

Beckenham-born Currey was honorary treasurer for the Crystal Palace Skating
Club. His father Henry was also an architect and he designed St Thomas'
Hospital, in London, along with other notable buildings.

Frank Alpe

Born: 1847
CP career: 1868-74
Appearances: 20
Goals: 3

Frank Alpe joined Crystal Palace for the 1868/69 campaign, operating in
defence or attack.

The Anerley resident scored twice in Palace's biggest victory at the time – a 6-0
win over Rochester in February 1871. Working as a merchant's clerk, his only
FA Cup appearance came in the 0-0 draw with Cambridge University in 1874.

nabbed another for the Palace but Wanderers got a fifth to seal the win.

Palace fielded three Bouch brothers for the Boxing Day home clash against Harrow Chequers. The South Londoners took advantage of Harrow starting with just eight players by going in front with a Morten goal. When the missing players arrived, Palace stretched their lead with efforts from Alfred Lloyd and Fleet to win 3-0.

Perhaps the Palace players were still recovering from the festivities as they lost 1-0 to Windsor Home Park three days after Christmas at a wet Crystal Palace Park.

With an extra player, Windsor scored inside the first five minutes. Palace's 11th man (Fleet) then entered the fray after arriving late and they threw everything at Windsor but couldn't get the ball through the posts.

"The hill and the well combined tactics of the Palace reduced Windsor to act entirely on the defensive for the remainder of play, with few exceptions," wrote the Sporting Gazette.

"Now and then the ball would convulsively travel up hill, but nothing palpable came of it except the return of the mud-sodden leather to the lower goals."

January 4 was a busy day for the club with the full squad being put to use. Douglas Allport's side beat South Norwood 3-2 at home. Walter Dorling dropped out as he was "unable to find his galoshes" but CPFC still had 10 men to their opponents' nine.

"Upon commencing play it was evident that the home team had the best of it, and for the first half hour their goal-keeper had a sinecure," wrote the Norwood News. "In fact, had the soil been more congenial nothing could have prevented Heath from taking root."

Goals from Fleet, Thompson and William Stainburn put Palace in the driving seat before Norwood captain HW Wilson pulled one back. And when he added another with a shot just under the tape, "this turn in their affairs had the effect of inducing the Sydenham captain to inquire about time.

"And a spectator in a mackintosh, who was cowering under a tree a quarter of a mile off (probably the only living thing out of doors in the parish), having found his watch and made an inaudible remark, time was called."

Across London in Balham, Palace had one extra player to Clapham Rovers' 10 but were defeated 1-0, with Alfred Bouch skippering the side.

Meanwhile at the Kennington Oval, Morten, Robert Kingsford and Chenery turned out for London in their second fixture of the season against Sheffield. Chenery scored the game's only goal five minutes before full-time.

The London football team, likely photographed before the 2-1 loss to Sheffield in March 1873. Charles Chenery appears to be sitting on the far right of the first row and Alex Morten is believed to be sitting in the middle of the second row. Robert Kingsford and Alfred Heath are among the unidentified players

"Mr Chenery getting possession of the ball near the goal, kicked it through, low down near the junction of the goal post and the ground and quite beyond Carr's reach, and ultimately were declared the victors after a very hard fought contest... Mr Morten outdid all previous efforts as custodian of the London goal," wrote the Sheffield Daily Telegraph.

The following week, Palace faced Clapton Pilgrims and routed them 4-0 at home despite having two less players. William Allport (2), Theodore Lloyd and Fleet grabbed the goals.

Palace met Barnes on January 18 for the 20th occasion in a match between the "venerable supporters of the Association game," said the Field. "From the first the Palace had slightly the best of the fight, and when about twenty minutes had elapsed CJ Chenery after a short run, secured an almost unstoppable goal."

A Palace latecomer arrived and Barnes played on with 10 players until the end with the game evenly balanced. But in one of the scrimmages, the ball rebounded off a Barnes man and through his own goal to give Palace a 2-0 victory.

On January 25, Palace had a first-ever meeting with Leyton, where they recorded their best-ever victory. Leyton arrived in Sydenham with nine players, so Palace's Henry Champneys joined their team to make it an even 10-a-side game.

"Being two men short, [Leyton's] captain was requested to choose a man from the ranks opposed to him. He selected Champneys, who was artfully endeavouring to conceal himself in the background," reported the Sportsman.

Palace took advantage of a shocking Leyton defence by scoring seven times and Champneys turned out to be a poor choice, according to the witty match report.

"Their substitute, too, though valuable as a perpendicular player, yet suffered so frequently from compulsory prostration that his sphere of usefulness was abnormally restricted," it said.

Fleet was then swapped with Champneys after being on the receiving end of some Victorian banter and he soon scored for Leyton.

"Fleet, the condition of whose attire was giving rise to expressions of dissatisfaction among his associates, was transferred to the visitors, for whom he very shortly achieved a goal," it continued. Leyton replied again, but Palace got two more to record a memorable 9-2 success.

The same day, Morten's Palace beat Upton Park 3-2 away thanks to goals from Fry, Soden and Alfred Lloyd.

"The Uptonians mustered one more than their opponents, but they lacked the individual skill of the Palatials, as, with few exceptions, they were unable to pass A Bouch and WR Collins, who acted as backs for the latter," wrote the Field.

Surrey and Middlesex met at the Oval for their return match on February 1, with Morten's Middlesex running out 3-1 victors. Surrey featured Chenery, Alfred Lloyd and Fleet.

Allport took an 11-man line-up to Reigate Priory on February 8 and that ended 1-1. After James Kingsford put Palace in front, Reigate equalised when "Pawle after a good run down, made a hard side shot at the Palace goal, and following up again with vigour, he succeeded in charging the goal-keeper and the ball through the posts."

Palace hosted Clapham Rovers on February 22 and were defeated 2-1. With no rugby rules game on that day, Clapham picked four of their rugby players who were noted for their pace, said Bell's Life.

Theodore Lloyd

Born: September 7, 1834
CP career: 1862-73
Appearances: 37
Goals: 12

Theodore Lloyd was a Crystal Palace cricketer who appeared in the football team's early games against Forest in 1862.

The Croydon resident was the first reported club captain when he led the side out against NN Kilburn a year later.

Lloyd was influential off the pitch too, serving on the Palace cricket club's committee and he attended the fourth FA meeting in November 1863 with James Turner.

Lloyd enjoyed bagging goals and he was the club's top marksman in 1869/70. "Always played with his head, and set an example to his juniors," wrote the Sportsman in a game with Brixton. Earning his living as a stockbroker, he sits third in Palace's all-time goal-scoring chart.

Worcestershire-born Lloyd refereed the second official England fixture against Scotland in 1873, aged 38.

He is the great-great grandson of Sampson Lloyd II, a Quaker who was the co-founder of Lloyds Bank. He is the eldest brother of Alfred and Henry.

William Bouch

Born: 1847
CP career: 1869-75
Appearances: 30
Goals: 2

William Bouch featured in each of Palace's five FA Cup ties on the way to the semi-final in 1872. During that great run, he scored the club's second-ever cup goal in the win over Maidenhead.

Bouch, who was a ship broker, has chalked up the second highest FA Cup appearances, with nine. He led a Palace side to victory over South Norwood in 1872 in a rare outing as captain.

Born in Dulwich, he was a pupil at Forest School and could play at the back, half back or forward. Brother of teammate Alfred, their other sibling John played football for Forest School.

The Palace goal was kept intact by fine back play from Lawrence Cloete and goal-keeping of James Turner. Dorling then fired just under the tape to put Palace ahead.

Clapham equalised from a free-kick after Hutton had handled the ball and Henry Bryden got the winner for the away team. The Palace players even complimented him on his goal. Bryden would eventually win an England rugby cap in 1874. He 'scored' again but the Palace players disputed it for offside and it did not count.

That afternoon, a weakened Palace lost 1-0 in Camberwell to the First Surrey Rifles.

Palace thought they got the breakthrough when "after about twenty minutes' play, a desperate attack was made by the Palace forwards on the home goal and the ball was driven between the posts. But the opportune use of hands by C Kolle prevented the advantage being scored," reported the Field.

This roused the Rifles and they got the only goal of the match a few minutes later, and also hit the post.

At the FA's AGM on February 26, Douglas Allport was helping shape some of the game's rules. He spoke out against a proposal by Nottingham Forest that throw-ins could also be kicked in. His amendment that goalkeepers should be able to use their hands instead of just "for the protection of his own goal", was agreed.

In a trial match for the upcoming England friendly with Scotland, a Candidates XI faced off with a Wanderers XI at the Oval, on February 20. Allport captained the Candidates – which included John Vigne – and the Wanderers won 3-1. Morten was in goal for the victors and Chenery and Kingsford scored one each.

Reigate Priory FC still use their Park Lane ground, in Reigate, today and it is the oldest continuously used football ground in the world

On March 8, Morten was named captain for England and Chenery scored in the 4-2 victory over the Scots at the Oval (details are in the previous chapter).

A week later, in the final 'best of three' London v Sheffield encounter, Chenery and Morten were called up. In an entertaining affair at Bramall Lane, Sheffield went ahead in the first half, played under their association's laws.

With their favoured FA rules after the break, London equalised when Chenery set up Robert Kingsford to equalise. However, the majority of the 5,000 support went home happy after a late Sheffield goal saw them triumph 2-1.

"CJ Chenery, as usual, worked with unremitting vigour, and A Morten was unerring in his post of goal-keeper," wrote the Field.

With Palace's main men in Sheffield, Alfred Lloyd took a Palace XI to Balham where they were beaten 3-0 by Clapham Rovers. Palace fielded a player called 'G Looking'. Was this a pseudonym for someone with the name 'Good'?

Chenery remained up north two days later for London's match with Nottingham at Trent Bridge, which ended goalless.

Morten captained CPFC for the return against the Royal Engineers and final recorded game of the season. The fixture was due to be played at the Palace but the ground was closed and the venue switched to Chatham.

Palace were defeated 3-0 with the third goal being something more akin to American football or rugby. "A free-kick for handling was claimed close to the Palace goal, and from it a scrummage resulted, from which, after a severe struggle, a goal was obtained," wrote Bell's Life.

"All the Sappers, with the exception of their goal-keeper, rushing into it, and at last the Palace team were forced back, ball and all, through the goal."

Palace selected England's Alexander Bonsor who put in an impressive performance, despite being on the losing side. "No doubt the palm for the day's play ought to be given to Bonsor who played beautifully throughout the game," added Bell's Life.

Bonsor had scored on his international debut against Scotland earlier that month and a few days later, won the FA Cup for a second time with the Wanderers.

1872/73 Results
Oct 12, South Norwood, A, 2-1 (Fleet)
Nov 5, Forest School, H, 1-0 (W Spreckley)
Nov 7, Royal Engineers, 1-4
Nov 16, Barnes, A, 0-0

Nov 23, Upton Park, H, 0-1
Nov 23, Clapton Pilgrims, A, 0-1
Nov 26, Forest School, A, 0-0
Dec 7, Reigate Priory, H, 3-0 (C Kolle, Chenery, Cumberlege)
Dec 14, First Surrey Rifles, A, 0-1
Dec 18, Wanderers, A, 2-5 (R Kingsford 2)
Dec 26, Harrow Chequers, H, 3-0 (Morten, A Lloyd, Fleet)
Dec 28, Windsor Home Park, H, 0-1
Jan 4, Clapham Rovers, A, 0-1
Jan 4, South Norwood, H, 3-2 (Fleet, A Thompson, Stainburn)
Jan 11, Clapton Pilgrims, H, 4-0 (WM Allport 2, T Lloyd, Fleet)
Jan 18, Barnes, H, 2-0 (Chenery, Own goal)
Jan 25, Upton Park, A, 3-2 (Fry, Soden, A Lloyd)
Jan 25, Leyton, H, 9-2
Feb 8, Reigate Priory, A, 1-1 (J Kingsford)
Feb 22, Clapham Rovers, H, 1-2 (Dorling)
Feb 22, First Surrey Rifles, A, 0-1
Mar 15, Clapham Rovers, A, 0-3
Mar 22, Royal Engineers, A, 0-3

FA Cup
Oct 26, Oxford University, A, 2-3 (Armitage, Lloyd)

Appearances
15 – D Allport.
12 – Fleet.
10 – Vigne.
9 – A Bouch, Cumberlege, C Kolle.
8 – T Lloyd, A Lloyd, Armitage, WM Allport.
7 – A Thompson, Morten.
6 – J Kingsford, Chenery, W Bouch, S Hutton.
5 – Soden, Sparham, W Spreckley, Stainburn, Turner, C Barber, Dorling.
4 – Borwick, W Collins, Horne, G Manvell.
3 – Masterman, Saward, Heath, H Cloete, Morice.
2 – F Kingsford, C Bouch, H Hutton, R Allport, T Spreckley, McEwan, L Neame, L Hutton, D Parbury, W Cloete, E Scott.
1 – R Kingsford, Betts, E Manvell, Brockbank, Currey, Willis, Greig, Alpe, Bonsor, W Foster, Fry, S Parbury, H Cloete, Hooper, Smouch, Powers, Yerkins, Johnson, Robertson, Champneys, Cockerell, R Slaughter, Venables, Looking, H Scott.

Goals
4 – Fleet; 2 – R Kingsford, A Lloyd, WM Allport, Chenery; 1 – W Spreckley, Dorling, C Kolle, Cumberlege, Morten, Fry, Soden, Armitage, Lloyd, A Thompson, Stainburn, T Lloyd, J Kingsford, Own goal.

Neame gets new role

1873/74

Crystal Palace started the season with the captaincy shared between the veteran Douglas Allport and the younger Laurence Neame.

Neame enjoyed a solid start as skipper by leading his players to a 3-2 win at home to South Norwood on October 11.

Despite being a player short, Palace went ahead through Charles Chenery. Norwood responded with a chested goal from Borgnis and took the lead with a strike from Fletcher, as the CPFC players protested they were not ready.

However, Palace grabbed further goals from Walter Dorling and another from Chenery to wrap up a derby victory.

That afternoon, a CPFC team captained by Douglas Allport found themselves on the wrong end of a 1-0 scoreline at Barnes.

Palace opened their FA Cup account with a tie against the Swifts, on October 18, 1873. With some key men missing, Palace fell at the first stage again in a 1-0 defeat, at the Dolphin Cricket Ground, in Slough.

Goalless at half-time, "the change of ends produced some determined play on the part of the Palace forwards, notably of W Bouch and CC Armitage," reported the Field.

"But in spite of the most strenuous efforts of the visitors they were steadily driven back until a weak piece of play by [the Palace] goalkeeper gave M Jeans an opportunity of achieving a goal for the Swifts."

Palace's leading players Chenery, Alex Morten and Charles Cumberlege did not make the trip. They turned out for a Surrey v Middlesex match at the Oval on the same day, which the latter triumphed 1-0.

"Mr T Lloyd of the Crystal Palace Club, acted as umpire by mutual consent of the two captains, and his decisions gave universal satisfaction," wrote the Sportsman.

Now out of the cup, Neame's Palace took on Woodford Wells at home but were defeated 2-1 on October 25.

Woodford went ahead at the break, before Dorling scored with a shot that hit the upright above the keeper's reach and rebounded off his back and through the posts. The Essex side then nabbed a winner towards late on.

The match was the last reported game for 39-year-old Theodore Lloyd, one of the few players remaining from the original Palace line-up.

Over in Surrey that day, Douglas Allport's Palace had to borrow two Reigate Priory players and were beaten 2-0. The Sportsman wrote: "The tea fight that followed is said to have been more evenly balanced."

It was now time for the three-game mini series between London and Sheffield, with the first battle taking place at Bramall Lane on November 1.

It wasn't a good day for Chenery – and especially veteran custodian Morten – as the Londoners were trounced 8-2 under the Sheffield rules.

"A good deal is due to the [Sheffield] players themselves, who stick to the places assigned to them, and do not go chasing the ball whenever and wherever they please," wrote the Sheffield Daily Telegraph.

"It is quite evident that the Londoners either do not see our system of setting out the field, or do not sufficiently appreciate it."

CPFC played out a 2-2 draw with Upton Park at Crystal Palace on November 5. Upton Park won the toss and chose the Penge goal, but found themselves behind when William Maynard fired Palace in front.

"Emboldened by this early success the CP goal-keeper received orders to go in and win, but a short run down and good kick by F Maynard (William's brother) speedily caused the fall of the undefended Palace goal, and 'one all' was the score," wrote the Sportsman.

Upton Park took the lead for the first time and "this piece of ill-fortune roused the dormant Palatials to a sense of their position, and LH Neame taking the matter up warmly, was only to be appeased by a goal, which was well deserved.

"Favoured by approaching darkness the Upton goal-keeper, artfully disguised in a Palace jersey, was now discovered insidiously working forward.

"And it is impossible to estimate the number of goals which would undoubtedly have resulted from his machinations had not some terror-stricken player shouted 'Time!'. A general stampede towards the pavilion was the result, and the match was left drawn."

The Sportsman picked out Palace's Charles Morice, adding: "Morice, as usual, was

Cuthbert Ottaway

Born: July 19, 1850
CP career: 1872
Appearances: 2

Cuthbert Ottaway is regarded as the finest athlete of his era, representing Oxford University with distinction at five sports.

In early 1872, Crystal Palace 'borrowed' the Oxford University captain for their FA Cup ties against the Wanderers and Royal Engineers, where "some good runs by Ottaway were much applauded by the spectators."

On returning to Oxford, the Dover-born front man became England's first-ever skipper in their inaugural international against Scotland. He was noted for his speed and dribbling ability at a time before football engaged in passing.

"As a forward he certainly can hold his own against all rivals," said the 1873 Football Annual. Ottaway was an FA Cup finalist with Oxford University in 1873 and returned with the team a year later to lift the cup.

He was unable to repeat the trick when he helped Old Etonians to the final in 1875. He suffered an ankle injury and was injured for the replay which the Old Boys lost.

The former Eton pupil was a Middlesex, Kent and MCC cricketer, had opened the batting with WG Grace, and also excelled at athletics, real tennis and rackets.

A barrister by profession, he died from pneumonia in 1878, aged just 27, caught on a night out dancing.

Alfred Bouch

Born: 1851
CP career: 1871-73
Appearances: 18

Alfred Bouch came into the side for the 1870/71 campaign, playing at the back. Both of his FA Cup appearances against Royal Engineers and Oxford University in 1872 ended in defeat.

A student at Forest School and then Rossall, he captained a second Palace XI that travelled to Clapham Rovers in January 1873. Born in Denmark Hill, his brother William was a teammate and his sister Jane married Morton Peto Betts.

indefatigable, and worked on the swampiest side of the ground, when his muddy habitat and tortuous movements reminded one of a jack snipe.

"He was, however, less difficult to knock over; and those who remarked the roseate hues resulting from health and exercise, observed that, unlike Scolopax minor, he was often 'flushed' yet never 'settled'."

Three days later, CPFC were back on home soil with a clash against the Royal Engineers. James Turner replaced Morten in the Palace goal, while England international Hubert Heron made a guest appearance.

Hubert Heron

Heron would go on to claim five caps for his country, once as captain, and lift the FA Cup three times with the Wanderers.

The military outfit ended up too strong for Palace who were defeated 3-1 "despite fine dribbling of the home team". Captain Robert Kingsford scored Palace's only goal.

The South London Chronicle added: "The Engineers, who were entertained at luncheon prior to the commencement of hostilities, were not quite up to their usual strength – not in any way occasioned by the refreshment.

"Moreover, they were playing on a smaller ground that they are accustomed to, nevertheless managed to win."

Henry Hooper put away the only goal of the game off Robert Allport's assist in Palace's 1-0 win at home to Forest School. "Chenery, in particular, distinguished himself by his fine runs and his very close attempts at goal," wrote the London Evening Standard. There was an appearance for the brilliantly-named Augustus Oelrichs.

Hosting Clapham Rovers on November 22, Palace lost 3-0 and played with a man down: "Mr Parbury, who it appears was absent without leave," wrote Bell's Life.

While this was taking place, a below-strength Palace met Brondesbury at the Kensington Park Cricket Club, in Notting Hill. They had to borrow a player and lost 3-1.

CPFC travelled to Godalming on the Wednesday afternoon of December 3 to face Charterhouse and returned home defeated 2-0. Cumberlege did get the ball through the posts but it was ruled out for offside.

Palace continued to show the full strength of their squad when they put out sides for two fixtures on December 6.

Charles Eastlake Smith made his first recorded appearance in two years for a Palace

124

Charles Cumberlege

Born: July 29, 1851
CP career: 1872-74
Appearances: 23
Goals: 1

Charles Cumberlege joined the Crystal Palace Club in 1872 to take part in both the football and cricket sides.

Born in Karachi, India, Cumberlege moved to England as a youngster to be educated at Rossall School and then Somersetshire College before relocating to South London.

The Bank of England clerk, from Sydenham, scored the third goal in Palace's 3-0 triumph over Reigate Priory in December 1872. Cumberlege earned a call-up for Surrey that month and he made further appearances for the county.

He was listed among the Chief English Players in the 1874 and 1875 Football Annuals where he was described as: "Quick, and dribbles well, but should middle the ball oftener." Cumberlege also played two first-class matches for Surrey County Cricket Club.

He married Esther Fleet, who was the sister of Palace teammate George. Their son Barry was awarded an OBE for his service as a British Army Major during the First World War. Barry also played county cricket for Kent and won eight England international rugby caps.

George Neame

Born: September 6, 1855
CP career: 1873-75
Appearances: 10

George Neame was a bit-part player for Palace but was always dependable when called upon.

He played alongside his older brother Laurence in both Crystal Palace football and cricket teams.

George grew up on Duppas Hill, Croydon, before the family moved to Grange Lodge, Upper Norwood. The Harbledown-born defender also enjoyed mountaineering in his spare time.

He was a timber merchant in his father George's business, G.F. Neame & Co, in Gracechurch Street, London. George senior's cousin Percy was the first Neame to run the Kent-based Shepherd Neame brewery.

side that lost 3-1 at home to Maidenhead. AS Thompson got the Palace goal.

Meanwhile, Neame brought Palace to Leyton and secured an emphatic 5-0 victory. Leyton arrived at the ground late and Ernest Henry Bambridge made them pay by grabbing a hat-trick.

It marked the last reported game by James Turner who appears to have hung up his boots on his 34th birthday – 11 years after appearing in the inaugural line-up.

On December 9, Palace played out a goalless draw at Forest School, in Walthamstow. The frosty ground made it too slippery for either side to score.

There were goals in Palace's 3-0 home success over Gitanos on a mild December afternoon at the cricket ground. Gitanos were formed in 1864 and named after the Spanish term for Gypsies, presumably as they had no home ground. They primarily consisted of Old Etonians and Old Carthusians.

"The match was one of the most interesting and spirited that has been played this season, and although the Palace eventually won by three goals to none, the game was by no means one-sided," reported the Daily News.

"Chenery started the score with kicking a goal out of a loose scrimmage in front of the Gitanos' goal; then RL Allport following the ball up well sent it between the posts; and finally the ball was pushed through off Alpe's knee. Alcock, D and RL Allport, Chenery and Maynard were conspicuous for the Palace."

Five days before Christmas, Palace again fielded two sides in one day. Hosting Barnes, they recorded their best win over their old rivals with a 4-0 triumph.

"For the first quarter of an hour the play was pretty equal, until eventually the Crystal Palace forwards, settling down to their work, succeeded in scoring a goal from a

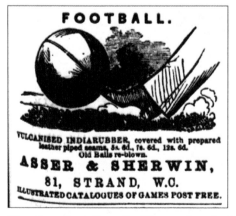
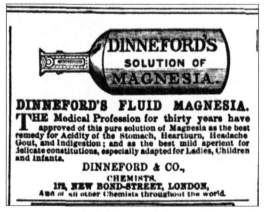

The Sporting Gazette (November 1, 1873) with ads for a London shop selling footballs and a chemist that provides bottles of magnesia to cure sickness

good bit of collective play and backing up," wrote the Sportsman. Palace added to the score with a brace from Robert Kingsford and a fourth from Eastlake Smith. "CJ Chenery and CF Cumberlege were always conspicuous, and assisted materially in the downfall of the enemy's stronghold," added the report.

But on the same afternoon away at Pilgrims, they only had nine players and it was not a surprise to see them lose 4-0 at Hackney Downs.

The Boxing Day fixture saw South Norwood make the short journey for their return game in Sydenham "witnessed by an immense crowd of holiday makers," reported the South London Chronicle.

Palace started with three players down and their opponents scored the first goal.

"The delinquents, however, soon turned up, and the Palace team were on their mettle, when, playing in capital form, they set to work in earnest, and made five goals off the reel without giving their adversaries another chance of scoring," reported Bell's Life.

Robert Kingsford got a hat-trick with Eastlake Smith and Chenery adding to the scoreline for a 5-1 CPFC win.

The next day, Palace again gave their opponents Reigate Priory a head start when they began their home game three men short. The Surrey outfit took advantage by going ahead but Palace ended up winning 3-2 after their late players finally showed up. Chenery was among the goals.

After London's 8-2 defeat by Sheffield at the start of the campaign, Morten was dropped from goal and officiated as umpire when the sides locked horns on January 3. Played under FA rules, Palace's Chenery kept his place in a 1-1 draw at the Oval.

Over in South East London, Palace's nine-a-side game also ended 1-1 at home to the

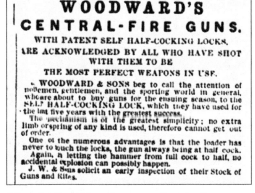
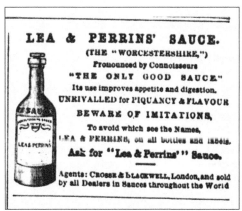

Also in the Gazette are adverts for a gun store (there were no legal restrictions on gun ownership in the Victorian era) and Lea & Perrins Worcestershire sauce

First Surrey Rifles. Palace were able "to score a goal through the instrumentality of CE Smith, the ball just dropping under the tape," said Bell's Life.

"Although the Palatians were reinforced by a later arrival, they were not able to increase their score." The riflemen levelled matters a few minutes from time.

Two weeks later, Palace were defeated 1-0 in the return match after having just nine players to a full 11 fielded by the First Surrey Rifles.

Frederick Maynard

With the Palace ground being "little better than a swamp", they were forced to switch their home fixture with Pilgrims to the base of the First Surrey Rifles in Camberwell.

Maynard brothers William and Frederick appeared together in the Palace line-up. Having joined earlier in the season, Francis Wilton scored in a 1-0 victory after the new Pilgrims keeper got sun in his eyes.

"Wilton broke away, made a splendid run down the ground, passed the Pilgrims' backs and goal-keeper, and scored," reported Bell's Life.

"The Pilgrims goal-keeper, embarrassed by his newness to office, and the sun's ardent glances, went out to meet Wilton, but he missed him and left their goal at Wilton's mercy."

January 24 was a packed day of football with Palace's away fixture against Clapham Rovers again ending in a disappointing 3-0 reverse.

Over in Sydenham, another Palace side lost a thrilling game 3-2 in the return against Brondesbury.

Meanwhile, Palace's leading players were appearing in a Middlesex v Surrey county match at the Kennington Oval.

Robert Kingsford, Cumberlege and Chenery were in action for Surrey and the latter's two goals were in vain ("the second hitting the tape smartly on its passage") – as they were defeated 4-2.

Major Francis Marindin of the Royal Engineers (pictured in 1892) became the new FA president

Douglas Allport

Born: June 6, 1838
CP career: 1863-75
Appearances: 107
Goals: 1

Douglas Allport was the backbone of Crystal Palace FC as player and administrator over 14 seasons and he holds the record for the most appearances.

Comfortable at the back, half back or in goal, the Penge resident became club captain in 1868. Allport replaced Palace teammate Walter Cutbill on the FA committee in 1871, where he served until 1874.

After the FA Cup competition was mooted, Allport proposed a sub committee to draw up its rules and jointly commissioned its first trophy.

He skippered Palace on their way to the 1872 FA Cup semi-final in its inaugural season, playing in each of the five ties.

Allport was on the England select panel for the second unofficial international with Scotland in November 1870.

He captained a Candidates XI in a trial match for an England showdown with the Scots in 1873 but missed out on the squad. At county level he represented Kent and also London in a match with Sheffield.

Allport was recognised by Crystal Palace chairman Walter Franks in 1872 for his outstanding service as secretary, treasurer and captain for many years.

He was presented with an ornate dining table centrepiece and elegant drawing room clock at the end-of-season supper.

He hung up his boots in 1874 but came out of retirement for Palace's last reported match against Barnes in December 1875, aged 37.

Working as a West India merchant in London, he often played alongside cousins William, Walter and Robert in the Palace side.

Allport was a keen sportsman, playing cricket for Crystal Palace CC and running for the Crystal Palace Athletic Club which he helped found.

Born in Peckham, he competed in the steeplechase and won a silver cup at a club one-mile race in 1869.

He was also a member of the South Norwood AC committee and played the occasional game for the Wanderers at football.

On January 28, Palace entertained Rochester and won 3-2 after a hard fight.

The ground was in a bad condition as Palace mustered a strong team. Rochester played with one man short as Chenery got among the Palace goals.

On February 14, Chenery and Eastlake Smith helped London to a 4-0 victory against the orange-and-purple-clad Nottingham. It was sweet revenge for London's 2-0 defeat in November.

Nottingham stayed in the capital for a fixture against Palace two days after and that finished honours even at 1-1. Palace went behind and the excellent Heron, making a rare start for Palace, levelled the scores.

"A rather fluky kick by Hubert Heron with his left foot passed just out of reach of the Nottingham goal keeper, and gave to the Palace a lucky goal," added the report.

Two weeks later, Palace staged an internal 'big side match' with a cup up for grabs. More than 40 club members dined at the end-of-season supper that evening.

When the FA met at the Freemasons' Tavern for the 1874 AGM on March 5, Douglas Allport stood down from the committee. However, Palace were still represented as teammate Alex Morten was elected in his place.

FA president Ebenezer Morley stepped aside due to business reasons – 11 years after founding the association. He was replaced by Major Francis Marindin of the Royal Engineers.

An FA committee selected Chenery for his third England cap and handed Robert Kingsford his debut for the showdown with Scotland, on March 7.

Now in his early 40s, keeper Morten was dropped but he was handed one of the umpire roles for the match at the West of Scotland Cricket Ground, in Glasgow.

England started well, according to the Morning Post: "No sooner was the ball in motion than the English carried it down to their opponents' citadel, Hubert Heron, Kingsford, and Chenery making some vigorous onslaughts, which for some time were successfully repelled."

A silver-plated tankard engraved: 'Crystal Palace Football Club, Big Side Matches 1873-4, Captains Allport & Neame'

Alfred Lloyd

Born: August 9, 1845
CP career: 1866-74
Appearances: 65
Goals: 9

Alfred was the youngest of the Lloyd brothers who played for Crystal Palace from its inception.

During an eight-year spell, the Camberwell-born stockbroker chalked up the second highest number of appearances.

Lloyd was selected for England for the first 'unofficial' international against Scotland in 1870 but was unable to play. The Croydon resident scored Palace's first-ever FA Cup goal in the 3-0 win over Maidenhead in 1871.

"A hard working, energetic forward; playing up well throughout," noted the 1873 Football Annual. Lloyd was picked for an FA Secretary's team that faced a President's line-up in a 'test' match to mark the brand new Association rules at Battersea Park in 1864. He represented London and also Surrey, scoring in a win over Middlesex.

Described by a teammate as "useful, but not loquacious" he is a descendent of Sampson Lloyd, who co-founded Lloyds Bank. He married Mary Spreckley – the sister of teammates Thomas and Walter.

Robert Kingsford

Born: December 23, 1849
CP career: 1869-75
Appearances: 20
Goals: 10

Robert Kingsford was a clinical finisher for Crystal Palace. He grabbed many important goals, including a fine hat-trick against South Norwood in 1873.

He was Palace's joint-top scorer in 1869/70 and 1873/74. His brothers James and Frank also appeared for the team.

Born in Sydenham, he was described as "a fast and invaluable forward" in the 1873 Football Annual. Kingsford, who worked as a solicitor, represented both London and Surrey between 1873 and 1874.

Listed as a Wanderers player, he was capped for England's 1874 game with Scotland and scored in a 2-1 loss. Educated at Marlborough College, the Palace cricketer played three first-class matches for Surrey.

Kingsford, 24, was listed as a Wanderers player and he put the visitors in front when he "received a fine kick on the breast and the rebound sent the ball flying beneath the tape," the report added.

However England, captained by Cuthbert Ottaway, conceded two quick goals midway through the international to lose it 2-1. Scotland's teamwork and passing game ensured their victory in front of a record attendance of around 7,000.

"What the Scotch lacked in weight was amply made up in swiftness and playing together power – a course which was splendidly illustrated during the game... They profited by each other's play, passing the ball, in several instances, in a way that completely astonished their opponents," wrote Bell's Life.

Meanwhile at the Oval, Palace came up against Gitanos – a team made up from the old boys of Eton and Charterhouse. A player down, they took a surprise lead and held on for a 1-0 win.

Maidenhead completed the double over Palace on March 14 with a 1-0 victory and a week later, CPFC were defeated 2-0 at Royal Engineers.

Palace finished their season with a heavy 3-0 defeat in East London at Upton Park.

Morten and Chenery had yet to put their boots away for the summer as they appeared in the final London-Sheffield match at Bramall Lane on April 4.

Veteran Morten was appointed London's captain and he left his usual goalie position to play outfield on this occasion. The first half was played under Sheffield rules, and after the hosts got the opener, it was cancelled out by Morten who combined with Chenery to nab the equaliser.

Both sides netted a goal each to make it 2-2 at half-time. Under London rules for the second period, Sheffield scored twice more to win a physical encounter 4-2.

1873/74 Results
Oct 11, South Norwood, H, 3-2 (Chenery 2, Dorling)
Oct 11, Barnes, A 0-1
Oct 25, Woodford Wells, H, 1-2 (Dorling)
Oct 25, Reigate Priory, A, 0-2
Nov 5, Upton Park, H, 2-2 (W Maynard, L Neame)
Nov 8, Royal Engineers, H, 1-3 (R Kingsford)
Nov 11, Forest School, H, 1-0 (Hooper)
Nov 22, Clapham Rovers, H, 0-3
Nov 22, Brondesbury, A, 1-3
Dec 3, Charterhouse School A, 0-2
Dec 6, Maidenhead, H, 1-3 (A Thompson)

William Maynard

Born: March 18, 1853
CP career: 1873-74
Appearances: 7
Goals: 1

William Maynard came into the Crystal Palace side at the end of 1873 having represented the England national team the year before.

Maynard, 19, started the first 'proper' international against Scotland in 1872 up front. He went in goal as a makeshift keeper for the second half and kept a clean sheet in the goalless draw. Palace's Alexander Morten was originally picked to play between the posts but had to withdraw on the day of the game.

Camberwell-born Maynard only had a brief spell with Palace, scoring in a 2-2 draw with Upton Park in November 1873.

He impressed in a 3-0 win over Gitanos a month later and the county court clerk also contributed to wins over Forest School and the Pilgrims. The 1873 Football Annual said Maynard was "a hard working player and dribbles well."

As a First Surrey Rifles winger, he claimed a second England cap in 1876, before joining the Wanderers. Maynard was living in East Dulwich and became a district registrar in 1903 when he moved to Durham.

Brother Frederick made the odd game for Palace and also enjoyed playing the rugby code. William's son Alfred won three caps for the England rugby team. He sadly died in the First World War.

Donald Smith

Born: November 4, 1848
CP career: 1869-75
Appearances: 19
Goals: 1

Donald Rigby Smith joined Crystal Palace during the 1868/9 campaign, helping the team to win four of the five reported matches he played in.

The Sydenham-based defender left Palace at the end of the season, but the banker returned in 1874 to play alongside his brother Charles Eastlake Smith.

Born in Sri Lanka, he grew up in Liverpool before the family settled in London. Smith moved Down Under and was secretary of the Australian Club, in Sydney.

Dec 6, Leyton, A, 5-0 (EH Bambridge 3)
Dec 9, Forest School, A, 0-0
Dec 17, Gitanos, H, 3-0 (Chenery, R Allport, Alpe)
Dec 20, Barnes, H, 4-0 (R Kingsford 2, C Smith)
Dec 20, Pilgrims, A, 0-4
Dec 26, South Norwood, H, 5-1 (R Kingsford 3, C Smith, Chenery)
Dec 27, Reigate Priory, H, 3-2 (Chenery)
Jan 3, First Surrey Rifles, H, 1-1 (C Smith)
Jan 17, First Surrey Rifles, A, 0-1
Jan 21, Pilgrims, A, 1-0 (Wilton)
Jan 24, Clapham Rovers, A, 0-3
Jan 24, Brondesbury, H, 2-3
Jan 28, Rochester, H, 3-2 (Chenery)
Feb 16, Nottingham, H, 1-1 (Heron)
Mar 7, Gitanos, A, 0-1
Mar 14, Maidenhead, A, 0-1
Mar 21, Royal Engineers, A, 0-2
Mar 28, Upton Park, 0-3

FA Cup
Oct 18, Swifts, A, 0-1

Appearances
17 – L Neame.
15 – Fleet, Masterman.
14 – D Allport.
13 – Cumberlege.
12 – C Smith.
10 – Chenery.
9 – Currey.
8 – G Neame.
7 – R Allport.
6 – Soden, Alpe, Dorling, S Parbury, R Kingsford.
5 – Oelrichs, W Maynard, Vigne, Armitage, A Thompson.
4 – Milverton, Wilton, Turner, Ford, Smithies, Viall, L Cloete.
3 – W Bouch, Champneys, Fraser, E Manvell, Morten, W Spreckley, Horne, J Kingsford, Heron, EH Bambridge.
2 – F Kingsford, G Manvell, C Bouch, Hooper, H Bevington, T Lloyd, Alcock, H Cloete, C Barber, F Maynard, Brockbank, F Abraham, A Cloete.
1 – E Scott, Clutton, Hubbard, Foster, Romilly, J Brown, V Williams, F Williams, R Abraham, E Abraham, Burt, S Brown, Rutley, Goodfellow, H Smith, C Kolle, T Spreckley, C Brown, Kingsford, Richardson, Craig, Morice, Stephens, Birley, W Cloete.

Goals
6 – Chenery, R Kingsford; 3 – Bambridge, C Smith; 2 – Dorling; 1 – Hooper, R Allport, Alpe, Wilton, Heron, A Thompson, W Maynard, L Neame.

Robert Smith

Born: May 1, 1848
CP career: 1871-72
Appearances: 4
Goals: 1

Robert Smith played an integral role in establishing football in Scotland.

He was a founder member and first captain of the Glasgow-based Queens Park – one of the few clubs to adopt the Association code north of the border.

Smith moved to London in 1869 to work for an oil merchant and joined South Norwood FC. The Aberdeen-born forward was selected for Scotland in the second unofficial fixture with England in November 1870.

Days after his third Scotland appearance, he lined up for Crystal Palace with his older sibling James against the Wanderers in November 1871. On his return to Palace, Robert scored in a 3-0 win over Scoonites in February 1872.

The Smiths were picked for the first official Scotland-England game in November 1872, as Queens Park and South Norwood players. They became the first pair of brothers to play together in an international.

Robert, who was noted as a hard worker and good charger, turned out for Palace at least two other times during 1871/72. He won his second Scottish cap in 1873 and emigrated to Wyoming, USA, that year to work as a cashier for a coal and iron company. His brother James sadly died of a stroke, aged 32.

Cecil Barber

Born: 1847
CP career: 1870-75
Appearances: 24

Cecil Henry Barber joined Palace during 1869/70 and was a consistent performer over five years. The insurance broker operated at the back or in goal.

Kennington-born Barber helped Palace to clean sheets in two of their three biggest wins: a 6-0 drubbing of Rochester (1871), the 9-2 thrashing of Leyton (1873) and 5-0 rout of Westminster School in 1875.

The Waddon resident was with Palace up until their final season and was jokingly described in one report as "the marine hairdresser (C Barber) who was never in more clipping form." Barber was also a Crystal Palace cricketer.

William Cloete

Born: 1851
Palace career: 1870-75
Appearances: 12

South African-born William Broderick Cloete joined Crystal Palace for the 1870/71 season after moving to London at a young age.

He lived in Penge while studying at Oxford University and helped Palace beat Brixton 3-0 not long after coming into the team. His brothers Lawrence, Alexander and Henry were teammates.

The Crystal Palace cricketer appeared for the Surrey Club and the Marylebone Cricket Club from 1877-93. Against Essex in 1877, he took 6-74 in the first innings and 6-48 in the second, scoring 60 with the bat.

A very successful businessman, Cloete *(pictured above in 1911)* was the managing director of a large mining company and operated in the border area of Mexico and the United States.

He and a fellow industrialist bought 1.3 million acres of land between Monterrey and Saltillo in Mexico.

When the Mexican National Construction Company built a railway across his land, Cloete became one of its directors. As a landowner, he also benefited from the railway accessing several of his mines.

Cloete was also a famous owner and breeder of race horses, with his colt Paradox securing a number of major wins, including the Grand Prix de Paris, and claiming second place in the 1885 Derby.

He struck up a close friendship with King Edward VII and said the king was a "good loser" after beating his horse in the Derby.

"He stood on his own merits and asked no favours not granted to the ordinary citizen," he said of the king to the El Paso Times in 1910.

Cloete had a modest fortune and went on to become one of England's richest men. He started a furniture business in London, and along with his vast interests in Mexico, he was the head of the steel firm Krupp.

Tragedy struck when Cloete died in the sinking of the Lusitania by a German U-boat in May 1915, while on his way back to London from the USA.

A coal-mining town he founded in the Mexican state of Coahuila adopted his name following his death and it is now known as Cloete or San José de Cloete.

All change at Palace

1874/75

The summer of 1874 saw a changing of the guard at the Palace.

Veteran keeper Alex Morten and 36-year-old captain Douglas Allport took a step back from playing, along with Theodore Lloyd, Alfred Lloyd and James Turner.

With these stalwarts now gone, Palace recruited new goalie Arthur Savage and Charles Eastlake Smith became club captain.

Savage impressed in between the posts for Crystal Palace in their first game of the season – a 1-1 draw against Clapham Rovers. Donald Smith got the Palace goal in Balham.

Away to the Swifts on October 29, Palace lost an evenly-fought contest 1-0 in Slough, with Savage repelling a number of attacks to keep the score down.

"The home team had some excellent forwards, and would have added to their score but for the capital goal-keeping of the Palace," wrote the Sporting Life.

Two days later, Palace crashed to a 2-0 defeat in East London against Upton Park FC.

Earlier in the month, Eastlake Smith, Charles Chenery and Laurence Neame represented Surrey in a 1-1 draw with Middlesex at the Kennington Oval. Morten officiated as umpire.

Palace were on their travels again, this time at Forest School, in Walthamstow on November 3. They lost 4-1 to the youngsters, with Eastlake Smith on the Palace score-sheet.

The three-match London-Sheffield series kicked off on November 7, with Morten dusting off his boots as an outfield player for the southerners. Played under Sheffield rules in front of a 6,000-strong crowd at Bramall Lane, Morten had a decent game despite the hosts winning 2-0.

It might have been a different scoreline had Chenery been selected, but he was helping Palace to a 2-0 victory at home to Gitanos at the same time. The nomadic club arrived with only nine men, so Palace lent them William Hubbard and Arthur Boosey to even the sides. George Fleet and Edward Barlow scored Palace's goals.

"Gitanos did not succeed in affecting anything, owing chiefly to the splendid play of

Ford, the Palace back," reported the Sportsman. "Amongst others, Chenery, Neame, Armitage and EP Barlow displayed some science."

Palace were paired with Cambridge University away in the first round of the FA Cup on November 14.

Morten was back in the side for a guest appearance with Savage again impressing by keeping a clean sheet in a goalless draw at Parker's Piece.

Not all the Palace squad made the trip as another team played a home game with South Norwood that day. Chenery (2) and Philpott were on target in a 3-0 victory.

Four days later, Eastlake Smith took 10 men with him for a midweek encounter against Westminster School, at Vincent Square. Palace borrowed a pupil to make it 11 each and the Westminsters soon got the ball through the posts. Palace objected for offside and the school reluctantly gave in.

In the end, CPFC were defeated 3-1 on a wet and slippery pitch, with Eastlake Smith the Palace scorer.

For the cup replay against Cambridge University on November 21, Morten and Alfred Lloyd started in a 2-1 loss. Palace surged into the lead when Fleet finished off an excellent run by firing home.

But in a game played in thick fog, the students equalised with a goal that would unlikely be awarded in today's rules.

"This advantage was soon neutralised by the Cambridge men, with a united rush, working the ball down to the Palace goal-keeper and driving him and it through the posts by sheer force," wrote the Sporting Life.

"Even play resulted for some time afterwards, until Simpson sent the ball again through the Palace posts, Morten not being able to stop its passage."

George Fleet scored in Palace's FA Cup defeat to Cambridge University

The return game with Upton Park on December 9 resulted in another defeat for Palace, as they lost 3-0 at home.

Palace's final outing of the year was against the Royal Engineers on December 12.

Charles Morice and Robert Kingsford came back into the side and they were joined by fellow England international Francis Birley, who had won his first cap against Scotland in March. A week later, he helped Oxford University win the FA Cup.

Palace could only muster nine players as Hubert Heron and JB Woolley failed to show up.

Despite playing with two men less, Palace put in a valiant display to keep it at 1-1 after Eastlake Smith had scored. However, the Sappers beat the offside trap in the final seconds to secure a 2-1 triumph.

England's Francis Birley

Bell's Life reported: "Hardly a minute before time was called the Royal Engineers were credited with another goal, chiefly owing to a misjudged cry of 'offside' which made Savage, the Crystal Palace goal keeper, relax his vigilance."

In the New Year, Palace picked up a comfortable 5-0 victory at home to Reigate Priory on January 9. This would be CPFC's last recorded game played on their own ground.

Skipper Eastlake Smith scored a hat-trick, with F Barry and W Allport one each in the rout. Crystal Palace cricketer Charles Fox was listed in the side. He would go on to play 80 first-class matches for Kent and Surrey between 1876 and 1893.

Savage's excellent displays in goal earned him a place in the London team that faced Sheffield at the Oval the following week.

Morten was appointed London's umpire and the capital's representatives ran out easy 3-1 winners against a depleted Sheffield side, played under London rules.

The match report in the Sheffield Daily Telegraph noted: "a new feature in this match was the appointment of a referee in addition to the two umpires."

Meanwhile, Chenery and Laurence Neame helped Surrey win their first-ever game against Berkshire, 2-0 at the Oval.

On January 23, Palace arrived at First Surrey Rifles two men short and were made to pay

Charles John MacDonal Fox

with a 2-0 loss in Camberwell. George Frederick Bambridge joined his brother Ernest in the team that day. George was the private secretary of Alfred, the Duke of Edinburgh and fourth child of Queen Victoria. His son, George Louis St Clair Bambridge, married Rudyard Kipling's daughter Elsie.

Palace locked horns with Brondesbury Park FC on February 6 and ended up easy 3-0 winners on a marshy Notting Hill pitch. The Sydenham club had an extra-man advantage with Chenery notching two goals and Frederick Maddison the other.

On February 11, Palace travelled to Vincent Square to play Westminster School and returned 5-0 victors. Eastlake Smith (2), Chenery and Robert Allport were the scorers in a strong team that also featured William Lindsay, Charles Alcock and Maddison.

Lindsay was a South Norwood player, who would get a Scotland cap in 1877 and lift the FA Cup three times with the Wanderers, scoring the winner in the final that year.

"Crystal Palace, evidently wishing to wipe out the disgrace of their defeat of last half, brought down as heavy a team as they could well get together, and amongst their number some names appear, which we suspect, were not those of strictly Crystal Palace men," wrote Westminster School's magazine.

"We made several determined attacks on their fortress, only to be repulsed by their impregnable goal-keeper [Savage]."

On February 13, the Kennington Oval hosted a trial match for the forthcoming England-Scotland match.

Chenery did his chances no harm by scoring for the 'Whites' in a 6-2 win against the 'Coloureds' who featured Savage in goal.

With Chenery and Savage missing, Eastlake Smith's Palace could only gather eight players for their trip to old foes Barnes that same day and were roundly defeated 3-0.

"The Palace being obliged to play with only one back and a goal-keeper, hindered the Barnes men from backing up as they wished, and there were frequent disputes about off-side," wrote Bell's Life.

A sports shop advertises rugby and Association balls in Charles Alcock's 1874 book Football: Our Winter Game

Laurence Neame

Born: January 14, 1853
CP career: 1871-75
Appearances: 44
Goals: 3

Laurence Neame began his football career as a teenager with Palace, coming into the side in 1871.

At 20, the Upper Norwood resident was given the chance to share the captaincy with his veteran teammate Douglas Allport for the 1873/74 season.

As a mark of their efforts, the duo were honoured with a silver-plated tankard engraved: 'Crystal Palace Football Club, Big Side Matches 1873-4, Captains Allport & Neame'.

Neame, who worked as a timber merchant in the family business, was rewarded for his fine performances by getting selected for Surrey in 1874 and 1875.

He scored twice in a week in November 1875 – against Westminster School and then with a long-range effort in Palace's FA Cup win over 105th Regiment.

After appearing in Palace's final reported game, Paddington-born Neame continued to play for Crystal Palace Cricket Club. Educated at Brighton College, his younger brother George was also a CPFC player.

Frederick Soden

Born: March 30, 1846
CP career: 1870-74
Appearances: 29
Goals: 4

Frederick Soden enjoyed a solid debut season, scoring in Palace's win over Upton Park and 6-0 drubbing of Rochester.

He was known as a well-mannered stockbroker, but also had a reputation for giving out heavy charges that were commonplace in the Victorian football era.

The Clapham-born forward's displays earned him selection for London in 1871 and 1872, then for Surrey the same year.

Soden was a Palace cricketer and played three first-class matches for Surrey between 1870-71. A graduate of Cambridge, he sadly died in April 1877, aged just 31.

A new rule change was discussed when the FA met for its AGM at the Freemasons' Tavern on February 24, 1875. The Sheffield Association proposed that the throw-in be replaced by a kick into play and this was supported by Charles Alcock. However, the idea was rejected by two votes.

Palace's Morten stepped down after one year on the FA committee and he was replaced by Palace club captain Eastlake Smith.

Back on the pitch, Eastlake Smith's team suffered a 2-0 reverse away to Pilgrims on Hackney Downs on February 27.

The Pilgrims took the lead thanks to an own goal by Palace keeper Savage who was unable to hold a corner kick and the ball rolled between the posts. Despite a CPFC fightback, Pilgrims added another one to secure the victory.

Palace claimed their biggest win of the season with a 7-1 trouncing of Leyton.

The South Londoners brought just eight players with them, but Leyton only had six and they went down to five after one of their men went off injured. So it was no surprise to see Palace run out comfortable winners.

On March 6, the Oval hosted a 2-2 draw between England and Scotland. No Palace men were called up, with Alexander Bonsor and 32-year-old Alcock on target for the English.

Palace finished 1874/75 on a bum note, with the final reported match ending in a 4-2 defeat at Forest School.

For the 12th meeting and the deciding London v Sheffield encounter of the season at Bramall Lane, the capital team won 2-0. It was the first away win for London in eight attempts.

William Lindsay played one Palace game in 1874/75

The Sheffield Daily Telegraph paid tribute to Palace's Morten who had to sit the game out for London due to sickness.

"There seems to be almost an intimate connection and association with our London friends, which has its own peculiar charm," it wrote.

"There was one jovial, happy face missing this time, the face of one who has probably ingratiated himself more deeply in the affections of the Sheffield team than any other with whom they have come in contact.

"The absence of that prince of good fellows, 'Alec Morten', was the only regrettable feature in the match, and we feel certain that all who know him will exceedingly regret to hear of his severe illness, and hope that he will have a speedy recovery."

George Fleet

Born: January 15, 1853
CP career: 1871-74
Appearances: 43
Goals: 6

George Rutland Fleet joined Crystal Palace at 18 and went on to become a mainstay of the side.

Born in Penge, Fleet became a famous singer, actor and comedian, known by the stage name Rutland Barrington. He's best known for his roles in the Gilbert and Sullivan operas from 1877-96 and enjoyed an illustrious four-decade career.

Educated at Merchant Taylors' School, he spoke about his time playing for Palace in his 1908 autobiography: Rutland Barrington – By Himself.

He said: "I had always been a very keen footballer, and at this time was playing for the Crystal Palace club, which, at its full strength, numbered some very good exponents of the game.

"Indeed, when county football was inaugurated and the first match was played at the Oval between Surrey and Middlesex, I was one of five players on the one side fighting three on the other, all out of our first team – a pretty good average for one club.

"What jolly matches we had too all round London, even going as far as Chatham to play the Sappers (a long journey in those days), who then had Vidal and Marindin playing for them."

Fleet had to give up playing after a knee injury affected his ability to perform on the stage.

He said: "Forest School was one of our most enjoyable fixtures, and the scene of one of the crises I have alluded to, and also my last match.

"On arrival I found that I had not brought my barred boots with me; but, nothing daunted, I played in my walking boots, with the result that I came down heavily in turning, my right knee going out and in with two cracks like the report of a pistol.

"Of course, I 'retired hurt,' but after a spell of rest went, rather foolishly, to work again, with the same result. I got back to town in great pain, but went to the theatre as usual.

"But when I had been knocked down by the Pirate King and should have risen in my turn and felled him, I had to ask him to help me up. He kindly did so, and I went to bed for three weeks. No more football after that!"

1874/75 Results
Oct 24, Clapham Rovers, A, 1-1 (D Smith)
Oct 29, Swifts, A, 0-1
Oct 31, Upton Park, A, 0-2
Nov 3, Forest School, A, 1-4 (C Smith)
Nov 7, Gitanos, H, 2-0 (Fleet, E Barlow)
Nov 14, South Norwood, H, 3-0 (Philpott, Chenery 2)
Nov 18, Westminster School, A, 1-3 (C Smith)
Dec 9, Upton Park, H, 0-3
Dec 12, Royal Engineers, H, 1-2 (C Smith)
Jan 9, Reigate Priory, H, 5-0 (C Smith 3, Barry, W Allport)
Jan 23, First Surrey Rifles, A, 0-2
Feb 6, Brondesbury Park, A, 3-0 (Chenery 2, Maddison)
Feb 11, Westminster School, A, 5-0 (C Smith 2, Chenery, R Allport, Own goal)
Feb 13, Barnes, A, 0-3
Feb 27, Pilgrims, A, 0-2
Mar 6, Leyton, A, 7-1
Mar 9, Forest School, A, 2-4

FA Cup
Nov 14, Cambridge University, A, 0-0
Nov 21, Cambridge University, H, 1-2 (Fleet)

Appearances
15 – C Smith.
12 – L Neame.
11 – Savage.
8 – D Smith.
7 – Woolley.
6 – Fleet, Vigne, Chenery, F Barlow.
4 – A Lloyd.
3 – E Barlow, Armitage, Morten, Ford, Masterman, R Allport, Keen, W Foster, Morice, EH Bambridge.
2 – Philpott, W Bouch, Soden, Currey, Viall, Maddison, Buchanan, C Barber, D Allport, T Spreckley, W Spreckley, W Maynard, Boosey, R Kingsford.
1 – Birley, J Kingsford, W Cloete, Wilton, W Allport, Alpe, Warrington, Borman, Thornhill, Elmslie, Brewer, Fox, Barry, S Smith, H Smith, H Solly, G Neame, Alcock, Lindsay, F Maynard, Cumberlege, Bouch, Lloyd, Smith, WM Allport, Richardson, Romilly, Way, Frank, Horne, Simpson, GF Bambridge, Longstaffe.

Goals
8 – C Smith; 5 – Chenery; 2 – Fleet; 1 – Philpott, Barry, W Allport, D Smith, E Barlow, Maddison, R Allport, Own goal.

The end is nigh

1875/76

Crystal Palace announced their fixtures at the start of the 1875/76 season and they appeared to be homeless again as all matches were scheduled away.

England international Charles Chenery was no longer playing for the club and his forward play and goals would be missed.

Charles Eastlake Smith remained as club captain and he got the new campaign off to a flyer by scoring twice in Surrey's 4-0 success over Berkshire. Palace teammate Charles Armitage also played his part in the win at the Kennington Oval.

On October 23, Eastlake Smith brought just eight players with him to Clapham Rovers for Palace's first recorded fixture of the new campaign. The lack of numbers cost them dearly as Rovers' two extra men helped them to a 4-1 success in Balham.

Away to Woodford Wells a week later, Palace arrived with a player short but held out for a goalless draw, despite one of their defenders hobbling off injured.

Peckham-born Charles William Burls, who played cricket for Crystal Palace and 17 matches for Surrey between 1873-80, made an appearance for Palace.

Charles Burls

"The Palace goal was subjected to numerous shots, though none took effect, as Wilton was in great form between the posts," reported the Sportsman.

"Soon after changing ends at half-time the visitors were unfortunate in losing the service of one of their backs, who was obliged to retire, having met with an accident.

"With the hill in the favour the Woodford forwards kept the Palace fortress in a state of hot siege, sending the ball on all sides of the post, but when time was called their efforts had been ineffectual, mainly owing to the judgment of the goal-keeper."

In the FA Cup first round, Palace came up against 105th Regiment in Aldershot on November 6, and Bell's Life reported an even encounter that finished 0-0.

"The Palace team penned their opponents considerably during the first half of the time, but no goal was the result, owing to the strong defence made," it wrote. "After a change of goals they still continued to press hard upon the 105th, though,

WH Smith's stall in the subway of the high level station at Crystal Palace, 1875

perhaps the ball was kept more in the centre of the ground, and towards the end of the game the 105th certainly had the best of it, two or three times dangerously near scoring.

"Both sides worked with great spirit; indeed, the play was so even on either side that it would be difficult to particularise."

While the replay was being organised, Palace journeyed to the Camberwell-based First Surrey Rifles, in a match played in heavy fog.

The Sportsman reported: "No sooner had the ball been started than the rain increased and fog began to creep all over... and consequently scientific play was out of the question.

"Up to half time the game was very even, and the Palace captain then wished to abandon the game, but two or three of his men and all the Rifles wished for a continuance, so the play was continued for about twenty minutes more, when it was agreed to leave off.

"Towards the end the Rifles, who certainly seemed far the most enthusiastic lovers of football, obtained a slight advantage, but no score was made, and the game left drawn."

Keeper Arthur Savage came back into the side for a 2-2 draw at Westminster School

Charles Smith

Born: 1850
CP career: 1869-75
Appearances: 56
Goals: 15

Charles Eastlake Smith is one of Crystal Palace's greatest goal scorers after two successful spells with the club.

He came to Palace during the 1868/69 season after finishing his education at Rossall School, in Lancashire, where he was captain of the football team.

Born in Colombo, Ceylon (Sri Lanka), to an East Indian merchant, Smith moved to Liverpool as a youngster before eventually living at Longton Grove, in Sydenham.

An insurance clerk by profession, Smith appeared in Palace's landmark first FA Cup game against Hitchin, in 1871, but the forward departed CPFC in the 1872/73 campaign.

He returned to the line-up the following year and his impressive displays earned him selection for London and Surrey, scoring for the latter against Essex in 1876.

Smith was named club captain for 1874/75 and he bagged a hat-trick in a 5-0 win over Reigate Priory that season.

He notched Palace's crucial second goal in the 3-0 FA Cup win over 105th Regiment in November 1875 and often played alongside his elder brother Donald.

Smith was an able administrator, serving as secretary of CPFC and also the cricket club, where he held the position until 1888. He was elected to the FA committee at its 1875 AGM after Alex Morten stood down.

His scoring exploits earned him a call-up to the England side for their clash with Scotland in March 1876.

Though they were defeated 3-0, he was among the players praised by the Morning Post who "played splendidly for England, but their gallant efforts were repelled."

A cricketer for Palace, his daughter Gwendoline Eastlake Smith was a major tennis star, winning gold for Britain at the 1908 Olympics and twice reaching the semi-finals of Wimbledon.

His cousin Gilbert Smith is known as one of the greatest England centre forwards of his era.

Crystal Palace won at Vincent Square, the playing field of Westminster School secured by Dean Vincent in 1810, and still in use today

on November 17 and showed "excellent play" according to the school's magazine.

"Till half-time, our [Westminster] backs were considerably bothered by CE Smith, who kept getting well away and passing them, and at length, after a very fine piece of dribbling, he scored the first goal for the Palace, the ball glancing through off the goal posts," it added.

The youngsters equalised, before Laurence Neame put Palace back in front off a throw-in by WH White. However, the school snatched an equaliser for 2-2 late on.

Palace sealed their place in the next round of the FA Cup with a 3-0 replay victory against 105th Regiment at the Oval on November 20.

"The Palace team soon carried the ball from the gas works end and down to the regimental goal, where it remained principally for the first half of the game, during which time the Palatians had secured one goal, kicked by Neame," wrote Bell's Life.

"Soon the Military fortress was the immediate scene of strife, and C Smith scored a second goal. From this time the Palace half of the ground was rarely visited, and when play had lasted just one hour EP Barlow added a third goal."

Palace ended a hectic November schedule with a 4-0 defeat at Forest School on the 27th, in Walthamstow.

Smith was part of the FA committee at Surrey Cricket ground that drew Palace out of the hat with the Wanderers for the cup's second round.

Palace's Augustus Oelrichs joined Charles Alcock of the Wanderers as the tie's

Alexander Morten

Born: November 15, 1831
CP career: 1865-74
Appearances: 52
Goals: 1

Alexander Morten joined from NN Kilburn ahead of the 1865/66 season and became a linchpin of the Crystal Palace side for nine years.

He went in goal as a late replacement for Scotland in the first 'unofficial' friendly with England in 1870, despite being born in Paddington. Morten was then chosen as an umpire for the second and fifth games.

Palace's deputy captain played outfield in the club's inaugural FA Cup tie against Hitchin in 1871. He then kept three clean sheets out of four games in goal during CPFC's run to the semi-finals.

Palace lost to the Royal Engineers but "the greatest praise is due to Morten, the duties of goalkeeper in this match being the most onerous," reported Bell's Life. A stockbroker on the London Stock Exchange, he won representative honours with London, Middlesex and also the South.

In an 1873 London clash at Sheffield, the local paper paid tribute to the stopper. "Mr Morten outdid all previous efforts as custodian of the London goal," wrote the Sheffield Daily Telegraph.

Despite previously representing Scotland, Morten was selected for England in the first 'proper' international against the Scots but he had to withdraw due to illness.

He made his England bow as captain in a 4-2 'official' win over Scotland at the Oval in March 1873. Aged 41, Morten is the oldest player to make an England debut and he remains his country's second-oldest player ever behind Stanley Matthews.

A profile on Morten in the 1873 Football Annual read: "Toujours pret is his motto when between the posts, in which position he is without a rival, never losing his head, even under the most trying circumstances. Has for many years rendered good service to the cause of the Association game."

A Crystal Palace cricketer, Morten served on the FA committee from 1874 to 1875 after replacing Palace teammate Douglas Allport. He acted as an umpire for England's battle with Scotland in March 1874.

The veteran captained London for their match with Sheffield the following month as an outfield player and he scored in the 4-2 loss. "Now almost retired from active service in the field, but as umpire is still held in the highest esteem," noted the 1874 Football Annual.

umpires. The Wanderers ran out convincing 3-0 winners at the Oval with goalkeeper Savage in inspired form.

"The Wanderers, who had mustered a very strong team, had it pretty much their own way," wrote Bell's Life.

"A goal was secured, when after a corner kick, Wollaston was successful in passing it under the bar. The goal-keepers had hardly reversed their positions, when F Heron kicked the ball through the posts, but the score was not allowed, on a plea of off-side.

"After this the Palace goal had several narrow escapes, but some time elapsed before F Heron and Wollaston each scored a goal in quick succession. And in the end, the Wanderers, who had played best throughout, won by three goals to none."

A week before Christmas, Palace travelled to Barnes to meet their old friends and fellow pioneers of Association football. Thirty-seven-year-old Douglas Allport came out of retirement to play in Palace's 3-0 defeat – their last recorded match.

The Sportsman wrote: "The match, rather contrary to exception, resulting in an easy victory for the home team by three goals to none.

"During the first half of the game Barnes were certainly hard pressed by their opponents, their goal on several occasions being in imminent danger, though nothing was scored notwithstanding the efforts of Armitage and Barlow.

"But after ends were changed Barnes had it all their own way, and the Crystals were

Forest School played their matches on the common in front of the school, where Palace were defeated 1-0 in November 1875

Charles Chenery

Born: January 1, 1850
Palace career: 1870-75
Appearances: 41
Goals: 16

Charles Chenery was Crystal Palace's all-time leading goal scorer and most-capped international.

He joined the club in the summer of 1870 after leaving Marlborough Royal Free Grammar School. Born in Berkshire, he worked as a solicitor and played for Palace mostly as a forward.

Chenery regularly appeared for London in their battles with Sheffield and he also gained representative honours with Surrey, including one game as captain. The 1871 Football Annual said he is "possessed of great pluck, a useful and persistent forward."

Chenery scored the third goal and "had worked hard and unselfishly throughout" in Palace's 3-0 FA Cup win over Maidenhead in 1871.

His stellar performances earned him a call-up for England's fifth 'unofficial' friendly with Scotland in February 1872, aged 22. Chenery kept his place in the side for the first official England-Scotland game nine months later and was praised for his "splendid dribbling".

Winning a second cap against the Scots, he scored his country's last goal "naturally and patriotically accepting it" in a 4-2 triumph in March 1873. The front man claimed his third and final cap in a 2-1 defeat to Scotland a year later to become the only player to be selected for England's first three fixtures.

"An excellent dribbler, never far from the ball, and always playing the game thoroughly," read his profile in the 1873 Football Annual.

And in the 1875 edition, he was described as: "A very hard working forward, playing up pluckily until the last, and always for his side."

The Penge native was an excellent all-round sportsman, competing in the sprints and steeplechase for London Athletic Club.

He played 13 first-class matches for Surrey County Cricket Club between 1872-73. In a match against Gloucestershire in 1872, he got out off the bowling of the legendary WG Grace.

Chenery was described as "a careful and trustworthy batsman, and is perhaps the best amateur in the Surrey team" by the Glasgow Herald. He played once for Northants against MCC in 1877. Chenery emigrated to Mansfield, in Victoria, Australia in 1878, to work on the family farm.

> Among other matches which of late have been played, one took place on Saturday last between Barnes and the Crystal Palace on the ground of the former club; although during the first part of the game the Crystal Palace pressed their opponents very hard they failed to score. During the latter portion of the match the home team, contrary to all previous expectations, completely turned the tables on their adversaries; and Dorling, Hadow, and Hudson, all succeeded in kicking a goal each, thus winning the game for Barnes by three goals to nothing.

Barnes v Crystal Palace match report, Illustrated Sporting and Dramatic News, December 25, 1875

good enough to allow Hadlow, Hudson and Dorling to kick three goals in quick succession.

"The Crystals now worked up a little better, till darkness put a stop to play shortly before time was called. Barlow and Neame did their best to make a good match of it for the Palace."

In Palace's fixtures printed in the Illustrated Sporting and Dramatic News, they were due to play at South Norwood two days after Christmas and were listed as "Crystal Palace Wanderers".

The Wanderers were called such as they did not have a home ground. Did Palace amend their name as they were no longer able to play at Crystal Palace Park? There is no known match report from this game and it's possible that it was postponed due to the weather.

Palace forward Edward Barlow and keeper Savage were picked for the London team's annual series of games against Sheffield on New Year's Day. The duo played their part in the Londoners' 4-0 victory, played on a boggy surface at the Oval.

No newspaper reports are available for Palace's remaining scheduled games (all away) in January: Clapham Rovers; the Wanderers; First Surrey Rifles and Barnes. And also matches fixed for February: Royal Engineers; Woodford Wells; Forest School and Westminster School in March.

Palace players, however, were in county action over January, as goalkeeper Francis Wilton helped Essex to their first victory after they saw off Berkshire 2-1, at the Dolphin Ground, in Slough.

Seger Bastard scored the winning goal for Essex. The Upton Park half-back also spent time as a referee, but is unlikely to have inspired the chant: "Who's the bastard in the black?!".

Arthur Savage

Born: October 18, 1850
CP career: 1874-75
Appearances: 14

Arthur Savage joined Crystal Palace in the summer of
1874 and made an instant impact with a string of
outstanding performances in goal.

The Sporting Life reported that the Swifts "would have
added to their score but for the capital goal-keeping of the Palace" in his
second recorded game.

Despite Palace's 3-0 FA Cup defeat to the Wanderers in 1875, the Sportsman
wrote: "Savage's goal-keeping was remarkable for activity, and his precision
throughout was exceptional."

Savage was described by the Athletic News as a "tall, well-built, bewhiskered
fellow... a very good goalkeeper with a strong kick." And in the 1875 Football
Annual: "A good goal-keeper, and a very powerful kick, might kick lower with
advantage."

Educated at the Royal Naval School, in New Cross, he worked for the India
Office. The Norwood resident caught the eye of selectors for London and made
appearances against arch rivals Sheffield in January 1875 and 1876, then for
Surrey against Essex.

Although Savage was born in Sydney, Australia, he was capped for England
in their 3-0 loss to Scotland in March 1876, aged 25. He stood in front of
wooden poles that replaced tape as the crossbar for the first time in this
fixture. "Savage played magnificently in the last half," wrote Bell's Life.

Savage returned to Australia, and after his experience with Palace, helped
introduce football Down Under. He was an organiser of the first reported match
in New South Wales under Association rules.

In August 1880, a newly-formed English Association club took on King's
School boys at Parramatta. "Mr Savage, an old international player, played with
and coached King's School," said the Sydney Mail.

Savage had joined the Australian military after working for the New South
Wales Government. He received his first appointment as lieutenant in the
Artillery in 1878, was promoted to captain in 1887 and major in 1893.

He retired at the end of 1902, due to ill-health attributed to the Boer war
campaign. A lieutenant-colonel of the Royal Australian Artillery, he "was of a
genial and unselfish disposition, and very popular locally," wrote the Sydney
Morning Herald.

England players from the March 1876 international against Scotland pose for a photo which is the earliest team picture known. Charles Eastlake Smith is standing in the centre and Arthur Savage is seated on the far left. Occasional Palace players Ernest Bambridge (seated, second from the left), Hubert Heron (seated, centre) and William Maynard (standing on the far right) are also in the line-up

On February 2, Smith and Savage appeared at the Oval for Surrey in a first-ever encounter with Essex. Hotshot Eastlake Smith scored the opening goal in a 1-1 draw between the county sides.

The forward was Crystal Palace's delegate at the annual FA meeting in February at the Freemasons' Tavern, in London, and he was elected to the committee.

"The hon sec. (Charles Alcock) detailed the great progress of the Association game during the last twelve months, instancing most prominently the remarkable hold it has gained in Scotland and its introduction into Ireland," reported the Field.

"And he had every reason to predict a still more material advance from the large addition to the numbers of Association clubs."

Palace were due to go to Vincent Square on March 4 to play Westminster School, but its magazine noted: "The match with the Crystal Palace fell through owing to the inability of that club to get together an Eleven to play us."

Walter Dorling

Born: June 10, 1855
CP career: 1872-75
Appearances: 14
Goals: 3

Walter Dorling came to Crystal Palace for 1872/73 and was a member of the side for three years.

The forward played in each of Palace's FA Cup ties in 1875/76, with the second-round defeat to Wanderers his final recorded game.

A week later in December 1875, he came up against his old teammates while playing for Barnes in what would be Palace's last-ever fixture. Dorling rubbed salt in the wounds by scoring in their 3-0 victory. The 1878 Football Annual described him as "a neat dribbler and good at the side."

Dorling's father was the clerk of Epsom Downs Racecourse and Walter grew up on the course grounds before the family moved to Woodside. He was educated at Charterhouse, later becoming a stockbroker.

His step-sister Isabella Mayson is the renowned Mrs Beeton. She would travel up from Epsom and rendezvous with Sam Beeton at Anerley Bridge station before they got married. Her 'Book of Household Management' is one of the most famous cookery books ever published.

Ernest Bambridge

Born: May 16, 1848
CP career: 1873-75
Appearances: 6
Goals: 3

Ernest Bambridge made the occasional appearance for Crystal Palace as he was predominantly a Swifts FC player.

Swifts were founded by his father William, who was a schoolmaster at Eton College and became the royal photographer to Queen Victoria.

Ernest had a memorable outing for Palace against Leyton in December 1873 when he scored a hat-trick in a convincing 5-0 win. He was "a useful and hard working forward," noted the 1874 Football Annual.

The Windsor-born merchant clerk was picked for England against Scotland in March 1876. Younger siblings Arthur and Charles also played for their country and they hold the record as the only trio of brothers to have done so.

Eastlake Smith and Savage were away on England duty that day where they won their first and only international caps in the friendly against Scotland. Played at the West of Scotland Cricket Ground in Glasgow, more than 15,000 fans turned out in the driving wind and rain.

The Scots scored three goals past 25-year-old Savage to wrap up a deserved victory in England's fifth official match. The Morning Post picked out Eastlake Smith among a handful who "played splendidly for England, but their gallant efforts were repelled."

Savage donned his umpire's outfit for the 1876 FA Cup Final replay, where the official is listed as a Crystal Palace representative. Wanderers beat Old Etonians 3-0 to lift the famous cup for a third time.

Eastlake Smith, along with Palace teammates Francis and Edward Barlow, were selected for London in the final of a 'best of two' games against Sheffield on March 25. Sheffield raced into a three-goal half-time lead and took advantage of a weakened London team to win 6-0. It was a sorry end to the season for the Palace boys.

1875/76 Results
Oct 23, Clapham Rovers, A, 1-4
Oct 30, Woodford Wells, A, 0-0
Nov 13, First Surrey Rifles, A, 0-0
Nov 17, Westminster School, A, 2-2 (C Smith, L Neame)
Nov 27, Forest School, A, 0-4
Dec 18, Barnes, A, 0-3

FA Cup
Nov 6, 105th Regiment, A, 0-0
Nov 20, 105th Regiment (replay), A 3-0 (L Neame, C Smith, E Barlow)
Dec 11, Wanderers, A, 0-3

Appearances
8 – C Smith.
7 – L Neame, Armitage, W Cloete.
6 – Vigne, D Smith.
5 – F Barlow, Ferguson.
4 – E Barlow.
3 – Savage, Dorling, W Bouch.
2 – Wilton, White, D Allport.
1 – Field, G Neame, G Boosey, C Barber, Morice, Burls, H Abell, Hubbard, Sedgwick, Ford, V Williams, Pittis, A Huggins, W Huggins.

Goals
2 – L Neame, C Smith; 1 – E Barlow.

Football carries on

When the new football season arrived in the autumn, Crystal Palace did not announce a set of fixtures for 1876/77.

The club itself, however, had appeared to be in strong shape with the 1875 Football Annual listing a membership of 70, which had been consistent for around a decade.

Officials were unable to arrange matches on their home ground and failed to fulfil their away games for the second half of the previous season. It coincided with the absence of retired Palace stalwart Douglas Allport whose leadership and organisation would have been missed.

Palace were no longer listed in the latest Football Annual as members of the Football Association. The players moved on too, with Charles Chenery and Francis Barlow going to the Wanderers, while William Bouch joined Upton Park.

Club captain Charles Eastlake Smith represented the Wanderers and the Anerley

A park photographer on Clapham Common in 1877. Crystal Palace came here for matches against the Clapham Common Club

based Hawks, but he was still a Crystal Palace cricketer where he remained honorary secretary.

The cricket club continued to flourish and put on a full schedule of matches over the summer of 1876. Laurence Neame, William Cloete, Frederick Soden and Percy Currey were also among those who stayed at Palace – but only as cricket players.

Football continued without one of its pioneering clubs and a pivotal moment came in February 1877, when the Sheffield FA agreed to adopt the FA's football laws.

A sticking point was the rule about throw-ins which were currently taken only at a right-angle by whoever picked the ball up first. The FA agreed the throw be taken in any direction by the opposing team who kicked it out – and this finally unified the football codes.

The FA Cup also carried on in Palace's absence as the game started to explode in popularity across Britain, with northern England clubs attracting thousands of working-class supporters. Some of the mill owners set football teams up for their employees.

Football was still an amateur sport and payment of players was prohibited by the FA, but some clubs began luring the best talent by giving them nominal jobs or discreetly giving cash.

In January 1883, the Athletic News revealed that Crystal Palace FC folded as they could not come to an agreement with the owners of their pitch in Crystal Palace Park.

This was divulged in a match report of a team calling itself Crystal Palace Rovers that played against the Pilgrims, in Walthamstow that month.

The writer says the idea of Crystal Palace Rovers was "to revive the past glories of the old Crystal Palace Club, which, in its day, was one of the strongest metropolitan societies, but eventually came to grief owing to a misunderstanding with the Palace authorities about their ground."

As with 'Wanderers' and 'Rangers', the name 'Rovers' has connotations of travelling, which indicates not having a home ground to play on.

Rovers were a team of Norwood players, consisting of old members of the Hawks, South Norwood, Clapham Rovers and Old Brightonians. No Crystal Palace Rovers match reports have since been found.

The line-up that was defeated 4-1 was: J Aste (captain), HW Williams (scorer), RA Walter, W Leete, PC Muspratt, H Knowles, N Leete, W Pitman, SA Fox, EJ Turner, H Reeves.

The Kennington Oval cricket ground (pictured in 1891) was the first FA Cup final venue

In November 1888, Eastlake Smith stepped down as honorary secretary of Crystal Palace Cricket Club and received a glowing tribute from a Palace official in Cricket: A Weekly Record of the Game.

It read: "Mr Smith held the office for fifteen years, and I can myself testify that no club has ever had a more zealous officer.

"He was an indefatigable worker, and it is no reflection on those who succeed him in the post to say that they will have a very high standard to reach if they hope to fill the responsible position he has vacated with the same energy and tact."

By now, after years of pressure from many of the northern clubs, the FA had agreed to embrace professionalism at a special AGM on July 20, 1885, with footballers now getting paid.

So what happened to the early amateur sides of the South who helped progress the game with Crystal Palace?

The Wanderers – who won the FA Cup five times – disbanded in around 1888 having not completed a full season since 1879/80. Many of its members opted to play for other clubs or their old boys' teams instead.

Barnes played in the FA Cup for the final time in 1885 and their last outing was a London Cup defeat against Ealing in 1894.

The last recorded fixture for Palace's local rivals South Norwood is a home game with Grey Friars in 1881.

First Surrey Rifles continued to play in the FA Cup up until 1886 and appear to have folded two years later.

Meanwhile, Aston Villa were one of the clubs in search of regular competitive football outside of the FA Cup and its director William McGregor proposed a new competition in 1888: The Football League.

Aston Villa's William McGregor

It was decided that each team would play the other home and away, with two points awarded for a win and one for a draw – and this was maintained right up until 1981.

The founding 12 members consisted of outfits from the Midlands and North with the London sides rejecting the proposal – possibly under the influence of the FA.

The teams competing were: Accrington, Aston Villa, Blackburn Rovers, Bolton Wanderers, Burnley, Derby County, Everton, Notts County, Preston North End, Stoke, West Bromwich Albion and Wolverhampton Wanderers.

Preston won the world's first football league title in 1889 – without losing a game – and they completed the double by clinching the FA Cup.

In 1892, the Football League added a new Second Division and the FA Cup continued to grow in popularity with more than 32,000 fans attending that year's final at the Kennington Oval.

However, Surrey County Cricket Club informed the FA that the ground could no longer be used for the football showpiece as it wanted to protect its newly-laid pitch.

The next two cup finals were held at Fallowfield, in Manchester, and Everton's Goodison Park, in Liverpool.

The FA was not convinced about the suitability of these venues and went in search of a London-based national football stadium.

Footie back at Palace

With no national stadium to host cup final matches, the Crystal Palace Company (CPC) spotted a lucrative commercial opportunity and spoke with the FA about building one.

One of FA secretary Charles Alcock's last acts before he retired after 25 years' service was taking the 1895 FA Cup Final to Crystal Palace Park.

The CPC removed the giant fountains (which had been costly to maintain), filled them in and the natural bowl made for ideal terracing around the pitch. Two large grandstands and a pavilion were also constructed where today's athletics track lies.

The FA was delighted with the result of the works and gave the company the green light to stage Aston Villa's match with West Brom in April 1895.

The CPC offered the FA a deal of £1,225 and a further sixpence for each person over 20,000 that went through the gate, which they gleefully accepted. On the eve of the FA Cup Final, the Shoreditch Observer was among the newspapers impressed with the new venue.

"The Crystal Palace directors have completed their new sports arena, which is probably the largest and finest sports ground in the country," it wrote. "It has been laid out at considerable expense on the site of the two large lakes.

"A substantial pavilion has been erected, containing luncheon-rooms, committee rooms, secretary's office, 23 dressing rooms fitted with hot and cold water and six bathrooms. The whole building is heated with hot water."

More than 42,000 watched Villa triumph 1-0 to lift the cup and the CPC showed its expertise in hosting a landmark event with a large crowd.

The FA Cup was stolen five months later from a window display in a Birmingham

The Graphic: An Illustrated Weekly Newspaper covered the 1895 final

football outfitter's shop where it was being exhibited and never recovered, despite a £10 reward.

An exact replica of the original cup that Crystal Palace FC's James Turner jointly commissioned in 1871 was re-made.

The success of the cup final inspired the CPC to bring a football team back to the park. On November 11, 1895, the Sheffield Telegraph reported there was the possibility of "a company being set up to promote soccer the following season at the Crystal Palace."

The company invited cup holders Aston Villa to an exhibition match at the Palace on November 30, 1895. The directors enlisted London FA president Nicholas Lane Jackson, who had served on the

A poster offering a reward for the stolen FA Cup

FA's committee and founded Corinthian FC, to put together a football team.

Corinthians were a famous London amateur club formed in 1882 and their global tours are credited with having popularised football around the world. Foreign clubs adopted their name and they are the inspiration behind Real Madrid's all-white strip. Between 1882 and 1936, they had 76 players capped for England.

"The Corinthians furnished the majority of the eleven which represented the newly formed Crystal Palace FC," wrote the Sporting Life.

It included England's Vaughan Lodge, Arthur Henfrey, Hugh Stanbrough and Robert Topham. The Evening Star added that: "JE Grievson (Framlingham College) was selected for the new Crystal Palace Club against Aston Villa."

Playing a 2-3-5 formation in their colours of blue and white, Palace started the game against Villa under the cosh. However, they went ahead against the run of play through Joseph Gettins.

Villa responded twice, but Palace's Austin Nicholson Guy pegged it back to 2-2 at the break. Stanbrough put Palace into a surprise 3-2 lead just after changing ends. However, the professional outfit's superior fitness shone through and they scored five more goals to win 7-3.

Hugh Stanbrough

A view of the new football ground at Crystal Palace during the FA Cup Final between Aston Villa and West Brom on April 20, 1895. Match programme, below

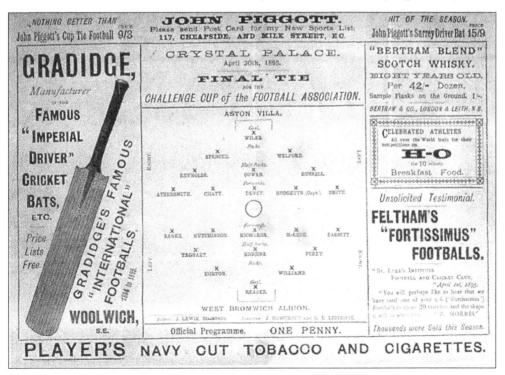

Palace: Turnbull, Lodge, McGahey, Henfrey, Grieveson, Alexander, Gettins, Stanbrough, Guy, Topham, Hewitt.

The match programme card mentions further Crystal Palace home fixtures against Sheffield United and Sheffield Wednesday in January 1896.

However, Old Carthusians replaced Palace as United's opponents "owing to the inability of [Palace] to secure a strong team," reported The Field.

Then Wednesday played Swindon at Crystal Palace instead as "cup ties and other things prevented the Crystal Palace from getting up a good side for this afternoon," said the Morning Post.

Many Corinthians were unavailable as they were playing elsewhere. The CPC only managed to stage one game – but that didn't put them off.

England's Vaughan Lodge

The programme for the Crystal Palace v Aston Villa match in November 1895

More exhibition games

There was speculation that the Crystal Palace Company was now looking to form a new professional team.

"When the extensive piece of turf was laid down for football and other games, it was rumoured that the Palace were about to organise a professional team and play all comers," reported The Graphic newspaper.

"This has probably not proved an easy task, for I think I am quite correct in stating that such was, and is, the intention of the Company. Experience has, no doubt, taught the directors that nothing but the best is of use as a public attraction; and the best professional talent is not obtainable at a moment's notice."

Regular matches were now hosted at the Crystal Palace arena, including Middlesex v Sussex in March 1896 and Nottingham Forest v Dundee the following month.

The Company managed to see off rival bids from Sheffield United, Fallowfield, Everton and Leeds FC's Headingley ground to stage the 1896 FA Cup Final.

A committee presided over by FA veteran Ebenezer Morley granted the showpiece to Palace again as a record attendance of 48,836 watched Sheffield Wednesday beat Wolves 2-1.

The Palace directors arranged matches against the cup finalists Wednesday and Wolves, plus fellow pro sides Derby, Bolton, Dundee, Nottingham Forest and Small Heath for the 1896/97 campaign.

First up was a match against a team representing the German Football Association on September 5, 1896.

The all-star Palace XI included a trio of Wreford-Brown brothers Claude, Oswald and England captain Charles, plus fellow international Hugh Stanbrough.

Gilbert Smith – a cousin of former Palace star Charles Eastlake Smith – was another international and is often referred to as "the first great centre forward". He scored six goals in Palace's resounding 13-0 win over the Germans.

Gilbert Oswald Smith

The full scorers were: Smith (6), Stanbrough (3), Taylor (2), Francis and CL Wreford-Brown.

Palace: Stout, O Wreford-Brown, Vidal, Francis, Dundas, Taylor, Stanbrough, G Smith, CL Wreford-Brown, Ryder, C Wreford-Brown.

It is claimed that Charles Wreford-Brown was the man who invented the word 'soccer'.

A fellow Oxford University student suggested they play "a game of rugger" (rugby) and Wreford-Brown replied by saying he would rather play 'soccer', shortening the word 'Association'.

It was a different Palace scoreline when FA Cup holders Sheffield Wednesday came to South London the following season on March 27, 1897.

England's Charles Wreford-Brown

Corinthian FC players were again borrowed for this game, including Cuthbert Burnup, who was capped for England and he was also a Kent county cricketer.

"The Sheffield Wednesday team brought their Southern tour to a conclusion with a match against a scratch side, including several Corinthians, at the Crystal Palace," wrote the Sheffield Independent.

"Unfortunately there were several defections from the advertised Crystal Palace team that had been selected to oppose the First Leaguers."

Wednesday triumphed 4-0 after goals from Bob Ferrier, Fred Spikesley, Alec Brady and Archie Brash and Palace keeper Harrison kept the score down with many top-class saves.

Palace: Harrison, Barrett, Ayres, R Foster, Bentley, Lecky, Burnup, Bosworth-Smith, Alexander, Gettins, Guy.

Cuthbert Burnup

Joseph Gettins

The home of football

The England v Scotland fixture is the oldest in football and the two nations have fought passionately since they first officially met in 1872.

England had staged their matches at the Kennington Oval but the vast new sports arena at Crystal Palace became their new London home after Surrey's cricket ground was no longer available.

On April 3, 1897, the Crystal Palace held its first England-Scotland international and the Scots were 2-1 winners in a tightly-contested encounter.

The Oxford-Cambridge Boat Race would have impacted the gate, but 33,715 fans were in attendance to watch the 26th outing between the old rivals.

The Scotsman reported: "Never before had the countries engaged each other at the Palace Ground, but the facilities afforded the public of seeing the match, were in every respect so complete that the contest appeared to be witnessed with comfort by all."

The FA Cup was of bigger interest to the Victorian football fans as just days later, there was a record crowd of 65,891 at the 1897 final between Aston Villa and Everton, which the Villans won 3-2.

The England v Scotland 1897 match programme

Back at Crystal Palace the following year, the showdown between Nottingham Forest and Derby on April 16, 1898, drew 62,017 fans, with Forest winning 3-1.

The Illustrated Sporting and Dramatic News said: "Than the sports arena of the Crystal Palace there is no better ground in England for a football match.

"Ample accommodation can be found for 80,000 or more visitors, while a decent space divides the nearest row of the spectators from the territory of the linesmen; and it is to the credit of the Palace authorities that the arrangements were perfect."

The Palace also hosted the predecessor to FA Community Shield – the Sheriff of London Charity Shield – a new fixture played annually between the country's best amateur and professional sides. The inaugural trophy in 1898 was shared by Corinthian FC and Sheffield United after the initial game and replay both ended all square.

A reporter from the Aberdeen Journal was impressed with the venue for the 1899 contest between Sheffield United and Derby, watched by a then-world record crowd of 73,833.

"The Crystal Palace football field is the finest in the country, having the advantage of being able to admit of a great many seeing the game, and of being at the same time picturesque and even beautiful," it wrote.

After the success of the cup finals, the Crystal Palace Company (CPC) was keen to attract more people to watch sport at the park and believed a new county cricket team would get the punters in.

So in 1899, it formed the London County Cricket Club and hired world famous cricketer WG Grace as secretary, manager and captain to assemble a first-class team.

WG Grace helped form the London County Cricket Club at Crystal Palace

A new pavilion and stand were constructed but it spelled the end of Crystal Palace Cricket Club. The London outfit was opposed to by members of Crystal Palace CC which had been around since 1857.

In 1900, the Palace hosted one of the FA Cup semi-finals, with Millwall and Southampton playing out a goalless draw, and 34,760 were in attendance.

Southampton won the replay 3-0 (played at Reading), but the south coast club were defeated 4-0 by Bury when they returned to the Palace for the final. The gate was an impressive 68,985.

The huge England-Scotland international returned to the Palace in March 1901 after Villa Park had hosted the previous home fixture.

A members' pass for use of a fine-dining club in the Crystal Palace building c1900

Torrential rain left much of the pitch under water and it was almost postponed due to the heavy downpour. The showdown finished in an entertaining 2-2 draw which was enough for England to claim that year's British Home Championship.

The record football attendance was smashed again, when Sheffield United faced Tottenham Hotspur in the 1901 FA Cup Final. A fantastic crowd of 110,820 watched a 2-2 draw and Tottenham won the replay 3-1 at Bolton's Burnden Park.

The 1902 event between Sheffield United and Southampton ended in a 1-1 draw, seen by 74,479. A replay was held a week later back at the Crystal Palace stadium, but before a much-reduced crowd of 33,068. United won 2-1.

Bury fired six past their 1903 FA Cup Final opponents Derby County to no reply, much to the delight of half the 63,102 at the Palace ground.

The Palace officials showed their expertise by yet again organising a large sporting event without any issues.

"There were most excellent arrangements made for the accommodation of the huge crowd expected, and these were carried out in a manner such as only the Palace authorities are capable of," wrote the Sporting Life.

Crystal Palace hosted its 10th FA Cup Final as Manchester City faced off against Bolton Wanderers in April 1904. City ran out 1-0 winners to claim their first major trophy with 61,374 in attendance.

Great Northern Railway cup final poster

The FA was pleased with the way the CPC had been running the cup finals and handed the company a five-year contract to stage football's showpieces and also two England-Scotland internationals.

The company began redeveloping the football ground and replaced the 10-year-old grandstands. There were two new stands holding 2,500 each, 16,000 additional seats and the grass banks were turned into terracing.

In April 1905, England met Scotland for the third time at the Palace and won 1-0 at the new-look stadium in front of a disappointing crowd of 27,599.

Scotland and Tottenham Hotspur forward John Cameron felt the English cared more for the cup finals than their national team.

"English patriotism differs remarkably from the other thee home countries, notably that of Scotland," he said. "The English regard internationals with interest, never with excitement.

"To this public, the event of the season is the Cup Final, the England-Scotland match is a secondary affair. Yet tonight in Scotland the rejoicing if the Thistles succeed will be overwhelming and of a national character. The telegraphs will be busy and they will not cease until every village and hamlet has enjoyed the news."

He was right as a month later, the FA Cup Final drew a staggering 101,117 fans as Aston Villa triumphed 2-0 over Newcastle United.

Action from the 1905 England v Scotland clash at the Crystal Palace

A red and blue future

The Crystal Palace Company (CPC) decided to forge ahead with its plans for a new, professional football club.

London County Cricket Club failed to inspire the public and it was decided to wind it down in 1904 as it was not profitable. Matches were overshadowed by the County Championship, while both cycling and motor car races attracted much larger crowds at the Palace.

The late Henry Gillman, who was the CPC general manager, had begun talks with the FA in 1901 about a new football club before he unexpectedly passed away. It was Gillman's idea to fill in the park's disused fountains to create a football stadium and he managed the subsequent cup finals with great success.

WG Grace, the company's sports director, asked his friend and London County teammate Charles Fry to help him set up the new football team. Fry was another fine sportsman, having represented England at cricket and football and equalled the then-world record for the long jump.

The new Crystal Palace FC would seek affiliation with the Football Association, use the cup final ground as its home pitch and apply to join the Southern League's First Division.

Football League chief William McGregor recommended that general manager George Cozens appoint Edmund Goodman as Crystal Palace FC's club secretary to get everything organised.

Goodman, 31, was an amateur player with Aston Villa and later became assistant to secretary/manager George Burrell Ramsay after a serious knee injury meant his leg had to be amputated.

Cozens, Goodman and Grace visited many London clubs and the success of Woolwich Arsenal, who were able to draw healthy crowds, gave them encouragement.

The FA did not like the idea of the CPC owning the cup final venue and the new football club. So Crystal Palace Football and Athletic Club Ltd was

Edmund Goodman

One of the elegant new stands built at the Crystal Palace

At the 1905 FA Cup Final, a then world record 101,117 fans packed the ground

created and it rented the ground from the CPC. Not that it mattered too much as the company became the largest shareholder.

"The opening season of London's new club at the Crystal Palace is being regarded with some interest. The club has leased the Palace ground for five seasons," reported the Edinburgh News.

Goodman set up a club structure and appointed a board of directors with Sydney Bourne named as the first chairman. The experienced Jack Robson, who was at Middlesbrough for 15 years, was appointed new manager and he signed the first group of professional Crystal Palace players.

Robson told the Illustrated Police News: "When we get [to the Southern League] you will see that we shall quickly take a position among the first flight. After two or three more likely lads, I shall have a team any manager in England might be proud of."

Palace had to settle for a place in the Second Division of the Southern League, and in the colours of cardinal red and light blue sleeves, were ready for their first match.

That came against New Brompton (now Gillingham) in the United Counties League on September 1, 1905 and Palace triumphed 3-0.

"A capital crowd watched the new Crystal Palace Club make its first blushing bow in the football arena," wrote the Portsmouth Evening News.

The maiden Southern League match came against Southampton Reserves the following day in their first fixture at the Crystal Palace.

Palace manager John Robson

Palace surged into a 3-0 lead but lost a thrilling encounter 4-3 – perhaps a sign of things to come for future supporters to experience.

Just 44 years earlier, on the other side of Crystal Palace Park, a group of gentlemen began playing an early form of the game that would end up becoming Association football.

Some of them may have been in the stadium watching the brand new CPFC. Without the enthusiasm and foresight of those early Crystal Palace pioneers, we might not have the popular sport and the club we know today.

The inaugural photo for the professional Crystal Palace team in 1905

Harry Hampton scores for Aston Villa against Newcastle United in the 1905 FA Cup Final

Crystal Palace Athletics Stadium opened in 1964 and has held many major international athletics meetings. The venue hosted the early FA Cup Finals and was also Crystal Palace's home ground from 1905 to 1915

Stats and records

Statistics are recorded from newspapers of the time but some data is incomplete due to match reports or other information being unavailable.

Crystal Palace

Formed: 1861
Disbanded: 1876
Colours: Blue and white jersey, (navy) blue knickerbockers and dark blue stockings

Grounds:
1861-64 – Crystal Palace ground
1864-67 – Billet Field, Penge
1867-76 – Crystal Palace ground

Summary of seasons

Season	P	W	D	L	F	A
1861/62	P2	W0	D0	L2	F0	A5
1862/63	**P2**	**W0**	**D0**	**L2**	**F1**	**A5**
1863/64	P1	W0	D0	L1	F1	A2
1864/65	**P8**	**W2**	**D4**	**L2**	**F7**	**A4**
1865/66	P7	W2	D4	L1	F5	A6
1866/67	**P3**	**W1**	**D1**	**L1**	**F4**	**A4**
1867/68	P6	W1	D3	L2	F5	A4
1868/69	**P18**	**W10**	**D4**	**L4**	**F22**	**A6**
1869/70	P16	W4	D8	L4	F10	A8
1870/71	**P15**	**W5**	**D4**	**L6**	**F16**	**A13**
1871/72	P28	W15	D4	L9	F29	A18
1872/73	**P24**	**W9**	**D3**	**L12**	**F37**	**A34**
1873/74	P30	W9	D4	L17	F38	A49
1874/75	**P19**	**W6**	**D2**	**L11**	**F32**	**A30**
1875/76	P9	W1	D4	L4	F6	A16
Total	**P188**	**W65**	**D45**	**L78**	**F213**	**A204**

Nicknames

Crystals
Palatians
Sydenhamites
Palatials
CPC (Crystal Palace Club)

Club secretaries

1863 – Frank Day
1868-70 – Walter Cutbill
1870-74 – Douglas Allport
1874-76 – Charles Eastlake Smith

Against other clubs

105th Regiment	**P2**	**W1**	**D1**	**L0**	**F3**	**A0**
AJ Heath's Team	P3	W2	D0	L1	F4	A2
Barnes	**P21**	**W5**	**D10**	**L6**	**F12**	**A12**
Bedouins	P1	W1	D0	L0	F5	A0
Brixton	**P4**	**W3**	**D1**	**L0**	**F5**	**A0**
Brondesbury Park	P3	W1	D0	L2	F6	A6
Cambridge University	**P2**	**W0**	**D1**	**L1**	**F1**	**A2**
Charterhouse	P3	W0	D0	L3	F1	A6
Civil Service	**P2**	**W2**	**D0**	**L0**	**F6**	**A1**
Clapham	P1	W1	D0	L0	F2	A1
Clapham Common Club	**P4**	**W1**	**D2**	**L1**	**F1**	**A1**
Clapham Rovers	P9	W2	D1	L6	F7	A17
Clapton Pilgrims	**P2**	**W1**	**D0**	**L1**	**F4**	**A1**
First Surrey Rifles	P8	W2	D2	L4	F4	A6
Forest	**P10**	**W1**	**D2**	**L7**	**F4**	**A12**
Forest School	P19	W5	D8	L6	F13	A22
Gipsies	**P1**	**W0**	**D1**	**L0**	**F1**	**A1**
Gitanos	P3	W2	D0	L1	F5	A1
Hampstead Heathens	**P1**	**W0**	**D1**	**L0**	**F0**	**A0**
Harrow Chequers	P3	W1	D1	L1	F4	A2
Hitchin	**P1**	**W0**	**D1**	**L0**	**F0**	**A0**
Kings School, Rochester	P1	W0	D1	L0	F1	A1
Leyton	**P3**	**W3**	**D0**	**L0**	**F21**	**A3**
Maidenhead	P3	W1	D0	L2	F4	A4
NN Kilburn	**P3**	**W1**	**D1**	**L1**	**F1**	**A3**
Norbiton	P1	W1	D0	L0	F5	A1
Nottingham	**P1**	**W0**	**D1**	**L0**	**F1**	**A1**
Oxford University	P1	W0	D0	L1	F2	A3
Pilgrims	**P3**	**W1**	**D0**	**L2**	**F1**	**A6**
Reigate	P6	W5	D0	L1	F12	A3
Reigate Priory	**P6**	**W4**	**D1**	**L1**	**F13**	**A5**
Rochester	P2	W2	D0	L0	F9	A2
Royal Engineers	**P11**	**W0**	**D2**	**L9**	**F4**	**A24**
Scoonites	P1	W1	D0	L0	F3	A0
South Norwood	**P8**	**W7**	**D0**	**L1**	**F20**	**A7**
Swifts	P2	W0	D0	L2	F0	A2
Upton Park	**P13**	**W4**	**D2**	**L7**	**F10**	**A17**
Wanderers	P11	W1	D2	L8	F5	A20
West Kent	**P3**	**W2**	**D1**	**L0**	**F4**	**A1**
Westminster School	P3	W1	D1	L1	F8	A5
Windsor Home Park	**P1**	**W0**	**D0**	**L1**	**F0**	**A1**
Woodford Wells	P2	W0	D1	L1	F1	A2

Club records

Founder members of the Football Association – 1863
Most wins in a season – 15 (1871/72)
Most draws in a season – 8 (1869/70)
Most defeats in a season – 17 (1873/74)
Most goals scored in a season – 38 (1873/74)

Best FA Cup season – Semi-final (1871/72)

Biggest home win – 9-2 v Leyton (January 25, 1873)
Biggest away win – 7-1 v Leyton (March 6, 1875)

Heaviest home defeat – 0-4 v Forest (April 5, 1862)
Heaviest away defeat – 0-4 v Pilgrims (December 20, 1873); 0-4 v Forest
School (November 27, 1875)

Biggest FA Cup home win – 3-0 v Maidenhead (December 16, 1871)
Biggest FA Cup away win – 3-0 v 105th Regiment (November 20, 1875)
Heaviest FA Cup defeat – 0-3 v Royal Engineers (March 9, 1872); 0-3 v
Wanderers (December 11, 1875)

Highest aggregate score – 9-2 v Leyton (January 25, 1873)

Player records

Most appearances – 107, Douglas Allport
Most FA Cup appearances – 10, Charles Armitage
Most international caps – 3, Charles Chenery (England)
Most county appearances – 10, Charles Chenery (London)

Most goals scored – 16, Charles Chenery

Hat-tricks – Charles Huggins v Civil Service (Jan 2, 1869);
Ernest Bambridge v Leyton (Dec 6, 1873);
Robert Kingsford v South Norwood (Dec 26, 1873);
Charles Eastlake Smith v Reigate Priory (Jan 9, 1875)

International goal – 1, Charles Chenery (England v Scotland, March 8,
1873)
Most county goals – 3, Charles Chenery (Surrey)

Longest serving player – Douglas Allport, 12 years (1863-75)

Appearances and goal scorers

Most appearances

Douglas Allport	107
Alfred Lloyd	65
Charles Eastlake Smith	56
Alexander Morten	52
Laurence Neame	44
James Turner	43
George Fleet	43
William Allport	42
Charles Chenery	41
Theodore Lloyd	37
Arthur Cutbill	35
Charles Armitage	33
John Vigne	31
William Bouch	30
Frederick Soden	29
Charlie Harvey	27
Charles Farquhar	26
Cecil Barber	24
John Sharland	25
Reginald Cutbill	24
Charles Cumberlege	23
Robert Allport	23
Henry Lloyd	22

Most FA Cup appearances

Charles Armitage	10
William Bouch	9
Alexander Morten	8
Charles Eastlake Smith	8
Alfred Lloyd	6
Douglas Allport	6
Laurence Neame	6
Edward Barlow	5
Charles Chenery	5
Alfred Heath	4
Percivall Currey	4
Walter Dorling	4
Arthur Savage	4

Most goals

Charles Chenery	16
Charles Eastlake Smith	15
Theodore Lloyd	12
Robert Kingsford	10
Alfred Lloyd	9
George Fleet	6
William Allport	6
Charles Huggins	6
Charles Alcock	5
Frederick Soden	4
Reginald Cutbill	4
John Sharland	3
Frank Alpe	3
Ernest Bambridge	3
Walter Dorling	3
Arthur Cutbill	3
Laurence Neame	3
William Stainburn	2
A Thompson	2
Charles Kolle	2
William Bouch	2
W Allport	2
Robert Allport	2
John Vigne	2
Edward Barlow	2
E Abraham	2

FA Cup goals

Alfred Lloyd	1
William Bouch	1
Charles Chenery	1
Charles Armitage	1
George Fleet	1
Laurence Neame	1
Charles Eastlake Smith	1
Edward Barlow	1
Lloyd	1

Most appearances by season

1867/68	7 – Arthur Cutbill
1868/69	18 – Douglas Allport
1869/70	13 – Douglas Allport
1870/71	14 – Douglas Allport
1871/72	17 – Douglas Allport, Alfred Lloyd
1872/73	15 – Douglas Allport
1873/74	17 – Laurence Neame
1874/75	15 – Charles Eastlake Smith
1875/76	8 – Charles Eastlake Smith

Top scorers by season

1867/68	2 – Charles Huggins
1868/69	4 – Charles Huggins
1869/70	2 – Theodore Lloyd, Robert Kingsford
1870/71	4 – Charles Alcock
1871/72	6 – Alfred Lloyd
1872/73	4 – George Fleet
1873/74	6 – Charles Chenery, Robert Kingsford
1874/75	8 – Charles Eastlake Smith
1875/76	2 – Laurence Neame, Charles Eastlake Smith

Club captains

1862-63 – Theodore Lloyd; 1863-67 – James Turner; 1867-68 – Walter Cutbill; 1868-73 – Douglas Allport; 1873-74 – Douglas Allport and Laurence Neame; 1874-76 – Charles Eastlake Smith.

Palace officials who helped set up the FA

Crystal Palace delegates present at the first six FA meetings which established the initial rules of Association football:

1. Frank Day; 2. James Turner; 3. James Turner and Henry Lloyd; 4. James Turner and Theodore Lloyd; 5. Frederick Urwick and John Louis Siordet; 6. Frederick Urwick and Lawrence Desborough.

Palace's FA committee members

James Turner – 1863-68; Walter Cutbill – 1864-71; Douglas Allport – 1871-74; Alexander Morten – 1874-75; Charles Eastlake Smith – 1875-76.

England internationals

3 caps – Charles Chenery
Scotland 0-0 England – November 30, 1872
England 4-2 Scotland – March 8, 1873 (1 goal)
Scotland 2-1 England – March 7, 1874

1 cap – Alexander Morten
England 4-2 Scotland – March 8, 1873 (Captain)

1 cap – Arthur Savage
Scotland 3-0 England – March 4, 1876

1 cap – Charles Eastlake Smith
Scotland 3-0 England – March 4, 1876

Unofficial internationals
England: Charles Chenery
England 1-0 Scotland – February 24, 1872

Scotland: Alexander Morten
England 1-1 Scotland – March 5, 1870

County appearances

Surrey
6 – **Charles Chenery** (Dec 1872, 1 goal; Feb 1873; Oct 1873; Jan 1874, 2 goals; Oct 1874; Jan 1875)
3 – **Charles Cumberlege** (Dec 1872; Oct 1873; Jan 1874)
2 – **Alfred Lloyd** (Dec 1872, 1 goal; Feb 1873)
2 – **Laurence Neame** (Oct 1874; Jan 1875)
2 – **Charles Eastlake Smith** (Oct 1875; Feb 1876, 1 goal)
2 – **George Fleet** (Dec 1872, Feb 1873)
1 – **Frederick Soden** (Dec 1872)
1 – **Robert Kingsford** (Jan 1874)
1 – **John Cockerell** (Jan 1868)
1 – **James Turner** (Jan 1868)
1 – **Arthur Savage** (Feb 1876)
1 – **Charles Armitage** (Oct 1875)

Goals: Chenery 3; Lloyd 1; Eastlake Smith 1

Kent
1 – **Douglas Allport** (Jan 1868)
1 – **Walter Cutbill** (Jan 1868)
1 – **AC Chamberlin** (Jan 1868)

Middlesex
1 – **Alexander Morten** (Dec 1872; Feb 1873; Oct 1873)

Essex
1 – **Francis Wilton** (Jan 1876)

Surrey & Kent
1 – **John Cockerell** (Nov 1867)
1 – **Walter Cutbill** (Nov 1867)

London
10 – **Charles Chenery** (Dec 1871; Jan 1872; Nov 1872; Jan 1873, 1 goal; Mar 1873; Mar 1873; Nov 1873; Jan 1874; Feb 1874; Apr 1874)
8 – **Alexander Morten** (Jan 1872; Mar 1872; Nov 1872; Jan 1873; Mar 1873; Nov 1873; Apr 1874, 1 goal; Nov 1874)
2 – **Arthur Savage** (Jan 1875; Jan 1876)
2 – **Frederick Soden** (Dec 1871; Mar 1872)
2 – **Edward Barlow** (Jan 1876, Mar 1876)
1 – **Robert Kingsford** (Jan 1873)
1 – **Charles Eastlake Smith** (Feb 1874)
1 – **Alfred Lloyd** (Mar 1872)
1 – **Percivall Currey** (Dec 1871)
1 – **Douglas Allport** (Mar 1872)
1 – **Francis Barlow** (Mar 1876)

Goals: Chenery 1; Morten 1

The South
1 – **Alexander Morten** (Dec 1870)
1 – **Charles Chenery** (Dec 1870)

The World
1 – **Charles Morice** (Mar 1871)

FA President's Team
1 – **James Turner** (Jan 1864)
1 – **Walter Cutbill** (Jan 1864)

FA Secretary's Team
1 – **Alfred Lloyd** (Jan 1864)

Player records

Player name	Palace career	FA apps	FA goals	Total apps	Total goals	Pos.
Abbott, RW	1870	-	-	7	0	-
Abell, F	1869-70	-	-	6	0	-
Abell, Henry	1869-76	1	0	16	0	F
Abraham, E	1864-66	-	-	7	2	-
Abraham, F	1873	1	0	2	0	-
Abraham, R	1864-66	-	-	7	1	-
Akenhead, E	1870	-	-	1	0	-
Alcock, Charles	1870-73	-	-	11	5	F
Allport, Douglas	1863-75	6	0	107	1	G/H/B
Allport, F	1863-66	-	-	3	0	-
Allport, Robert	1867-74	-	-	23	2	B/F
Allport, W	1862-75	-	-	17	2	F
Allport, Walter	1868-71	-	-	3	0	-
Allport, William	1868-73	2	-	42	6	F
Alpe, Frank	1868-74	1	0	20	3	B/F
Anderson, JP	1872	-	-	1	0	-
Armitage, Charles	1871-75	10	1	33	1	F
Baker, C	1870	-	-	1	0	-
Bambridge, Ernest	1873-75	-	-	6	3	F
Bambridge, George	1875	-	-	1	0	-
Barber, AG	1863	-	-	1	0	-
Barber, Cecil	1870-75	-	-	24	0	G/B
Barlow, Edward	1874-75	5	1	7	2	B
Barlow, Francis	1874-75	4	0	11	0	-
Barry, F	1875	-	-	1	1	-
Bell	1862	-	-	1	0	-
Betts, Morton	1871-72	-	-	3	0	-
Bevington, Herbert	1874	-	-	2	0	-
Bevington, Timothy	1862	-	-	1	0	-
Bickley, W	1870	-	-	1	0	-
Birley, Francis	1874	-	-	2	0	H
Body, James	1870	-	-	1	0	F
Bonsor, Alexander	1873	-	-	1	0	-
Boosey, Arthur	1875	-	-	1	0	-
Boosey, GE	1875	-	-	1	0	H
Borman, AW	1874	-	-	1	0	-
Borwick, Alfred	1869-73	1	0	9	1	B/H/F
Bouch, Alfred	1871-73	2	0	18	0	B/H
Bouch, C	1872-74	-	-	4	0	-

Player name	Palace career	FA apps	FA goals	Total apps	Total goals	Pos.
Bouch, William	1869-75	9	1	30	2	B/H/F
Brewer, AA	1874	-	-	1	0	-
Brockbank, John	1872	-	-	3	0	F
Brother, HJS	1870	-	-	1	0	-
Brown, C	1874	-	-	1	0	-
Brown, JHO	1874	-	-	1	0	-
Brown, SW	1873	-	-	1	0	-
Brown, TL*	1869	-	-	1	0	-
Buchanan, WS	1875	-	-	2	0	-
Burls, Charles	1875	-	-	1	0	H
Burt, A	1873	-	-	1	0	-
Butterfield, H	1867-68	-	-	4	0	-
Burrows	1871	-	-	1	0	-
Capper, C	1869-70	-	-	5	0	-
Carver, SH*	1867-71	-	-	2	0	F
Cazenove, E	1870	-	-	1	0	-
Chamberlin, Archibald	1868-69	-	-	10	0	G/B
Champneys, HL	1871-74	-	-	5	0	-
Chappell/Maddison, Fred	1872-75	3	0	5	1	B/F
Chenery, Charles	1870-75	5	1	41	16	B/F
Chidley, TJ	1867-68	-	-	2	0	F
Cloete, Alexander	1873	-	-	2	0	H
Cloete, Henry	1873	-	-	5	0	-
Cloete, Lawrence	1871-73	1	0	6	0	B
Cloete, William	1870-75	3	0	12	0	B/H
Cluff, J	1864	-	-	1	0	-
Clutton, RW	1869-73	-	-	3	0	-
Cockerell, John	1865-71	1	0	16	1	B/H
Collins, F	1863-65	-	-	4	0	-
Collins, William	1870-73	-	-	5	0	B
Craig, CH*	1873	-	-	1	0	-
Crowther, TW*	1869	-	-	1	1	-
Cumberlege, Charles	1872-74	1	0	23	1	F
Currey, Percivall	1871-74	4	0	18	0	B
Cutbill, Arthur	1864-71	-	-	35	3	B
Cutbill, Edward	1862-67	-	-	6	0	-
Cutbill, Reginald	1867-69	-	-	24	4	F
Cutbill, Walter	1862-68	-	-	14	1	F
Daukes, Henry	1868-71	1	0	13	0	-
Daukes, Samuel	1869	-	-	3	1	-

Player name	Palace career	FA apps	FA goals	Total apps	Total goals	Pos.
Day, Frank	1862	-	-	2	0	-
De Castro, H	1870	-	-	1	0	-
Desborough, Lawrence	1864	-	-	1	0	-
Dodson, J	1865	-	-	1	0	-
Dorling, Walter	1872-75	4	0	14	3	F
Dry, G	1863	-	-	1	0	-
Ellis, WGF	1867-71	-	-	13	0	F
Elmslie, RW	1871-74	-	-	2	0	G
Farquhar, Charles	1867-72	1	0	26	0	B/H
Farquhar, W	1863	-	-	1	0	-
Ferguson, Murze	1875	1	0	5	0	B/H
Field, W	1875	-	-	1	0	H
Fleet, George	1871-74	2	1	43	6	H
Fletcher, JW	1870-71	-	-	8	0	-
Ford, W	1874-75	-	-	9	0	B
Foster, H	1865-67	-	-	6	0	-
Foster, Walter	1871-74	1	0	10	0	F
Fox, CM	1875	-	-	1	0	-
Frank, W	1874	-	-	1	0	-
Fraser, F	1873-74	-	-	3	0	-
Frost, H*	1871	-	-	1	0	-
Fry, E	1872-73	-	-	2	1	-
Gardom, ET*	1867	-	-	1	0	F
Goodfellow, CA*	1873	-	-	1	0	-
Gower, A*	1869	-	-	1	0	-
Greig*	1872	-	-	1	0	-
Grose, J	1863-66	-	-	7	0	-
Hammond, ER	1866	-	-	1	0	-
Hartung, FM	1869-71	-	-	6	0	F
Harvey, CC	1868-71	-	-	27	0	B
Head, Henry	1862-63	-	-	2	0	-
Heath, Alfred	1871-73	4	0	13	0	B
Heddle, T	1870	-	-	1	0	-
Heron, Hubert	1873-74	-	-	3	1	-
Highton, Edward	1871	-	-	2	0	-
Hooper, HJ	1873-74	-	-	3	1	-
Horne, F	1871-73	-	-	10	0	-

Player name	Palace career	FA apps	FA goals	Total apps	Total goals	Pos.
Hubbard, William	1873-75	-	-	2	0	-
Hunter, P*	1870	-	-	1	0	-
Huggins, AE	1875	-	-	1	0	-
Huggins, Charles	1867-71	-	-	15	6	F
Huggins, W	1875	-	-	1	0	-
Hutchinson, A*	1870-71	-	-	2	0	-
Hutton, HE	1872	-	-	2	0	G
Hutton, L	1873	-	-	2	0	-
Hutton, S	1872-73	-	-	6	0	B
Irons, L	1864-65	-	-	3	0	-
Jack, C	1871	-	-	1	0	H
Jackson, T	1862	-	-	2	0	-
Johnson, J	1872	-	-	1	0	-
Jones, FCP	1870	-	-	1	0	-
Keen, J	1874-75	-	-	3	0	-
Kingsford, Frank	1870-73	-	-	5	0	-
Kingsford, James	1869-75	-	-	21	1	B
Kingsford, Robert	1869-75	-	-	20	10	F
Knight, RL	1871	-	-	1	0	-
Kolle, Charles	1870-73	-	-	19	2	F
Kolle, James	1867-71	-	-	3	0	-
Leete, B	1870	-	-	1	0	-
Lindsay, William	1875	-	-	1	0	B
Lintott, A	1868-69	-	-	3	0	-
Lintott, H	1870-71	-	-	3	0	-
Lloyd, Alfred	1862-74	6	1	65	9	F
Lloyd, Henry	1862-69	-	-	22	1	-
Lloyd, Robert	1862	-	-	1	0	-
Lloyd, Theodore	1862-73	1	0	37	12	F
Longstaffe, AP*	1874	-	-	1	0	-
Looking, G	1873	-	-	1	0	-
Luscombe, Francis	1869-70	-		6	1	F
Mann, LH	1871	-	-	1	0	-
Mann, WW	1870	-	-	1	0	-
Manvell, Edward	1869-73	-	-	7	0	-
Manvell, GS	1869-74	-	-	19	0	B/F

Player name	Palace career	FA apps	FA goals	Total apps	Total goals	Pos.
Masterman, HC	1873-74	1	0	21	0	G/B
Maynard, Frederick	1874	-	-	3	0	-
Maynard, William	1873-74	-	-	7	1	F
McEwan, G	1872-73	-	-	2	0	-
Medwin	1862	-	-	1	0	-
Melhuish, C	1865	-	-	2	1	-
Milverton, FB	1873	-	-	4	0	-
Montresor	1867	-	-	2	0	-
Moore, OWE	1870	-	-	1	0	-
Morice, Charles	1871-75	-	-	11	0	F
Morris, F	1864-70	-	-	4	0	F
Morten, Alexander	1865-74	8	0	52	1	G
Morton, MT	1871	-	-	1	0	F
Mosted, A	1869	-	-	1	0	-
Neame, George	1873-75	-	-	10	0	B
Neame, Laurence	1871-75	6	1	44	3	H/F
Noakes, Wickham	1862	-	-	1	0	-
Oelrichs, Augustus	1873	-	-	5	0	G
Ormiston, Phil	1870	-	-	1	0	-
Ottaway, Cuthbert	1872	2	0	2	0	F
Paine, T	1863	-	-	1	0	-
Parbury, D	1873	-	-	2	0	-
Parbury, SW	1873-74	-	-	7	0	-
Parr, George	1868-70	-	-	14	0	-
Parr, William	1867-69	-	-	8	0	G/B
Phelps	1862	-	-	1	0	-
Philpott, CH	1874-75	-	-	2	1	F
Piper, R	1871	-	-	3	0	-
Pittis, CE	1875	-	-	1	0	-
Poole, FG*	1869	-	-	1	0	B
Powers, SH*	1872	-	-	1	0	-
Rawlinson, WE	1871	-	-	1	0	-
Rhode, J	1864-65	-	-	5	0	-
Richardson, BE*	1873	-	-	1	0	-
Richardson	1874	-	-	1	0	-
Robertson, J	1872	-	-	1	0	-
Romilly, JJ	1874	-	-	2	0	-

Player name	Palace career	FA apps	FA goals	Total apps	Total goals	Pos.
Rouquette, Philip	1872	3	0	3	0	B
Rutley, H	1873	-	-	1	0	-
Rowsell	1865	-	-	1	1	-
Savage, Arthur	1874-75	4	0	14	0	G
Saward, Arthur	1866-73	-	-	8	0	-
Saxton, P	1870	-	-	1	0	-
Scott, B	1868	-	-	1	0	-
Scott, EF	1869-73	-	-	14	0	G/B/H
Scott, HJ	1870-72	-	-	3	0	B
Sedgwick, EK	1875	-	-	1	0	-
Sharland, John	1862-71	-	-	25	3	F
Simpson, D	1875	-	-	1	0	-
Slater, A	1869	-	-	1	0	-
Slaughter, J	1871	-	-	1	0	-
Slaughter, R	1872	-	-	1	0	-
Smith, Charles E	1869-75	8	1	56	15	F
Smith, Donald	1869-75	2	0	19	1	B
Smith, H le B	1875	-	-	1	0	-
Smith, H*	1869	-	-	2	0	B
Smith, James	1871-72	-	-	2	0	-
Smith, Robert	1871-72	-	-	4	1	F
Smith, S le B	1875	-	-	1	0	-
Smithies, HE	1873-74	-	-	4	0	-
Smouch, A	1872	-	-	1	0	-
Soden, Frederick	1870-74	3	0	29	4	F
Solly, RH	1869	-	-	1	0	-
Solly, Henry	1875	-	-	1	0	-
Sparham, HH	1872-73	-	-	5	0	F
Sparham, W	1871	-	-	1	0	F
Spreckley, Thomas	1870-74	3	0	19	0	F
Spreckley, Walter	1870-74	-	-	12	1	-
Stainburn, William	1869-73	-	-	15	2	-
Stephens, TH	1874	-	-	1	0	-
Stephenson, R*	1865	-	-	1	0	-
Stevens, HV	1870-71	-	-	2	0	-
Stone, EM	1868	-	-	3	0	F
Tebbutt, A	1865	-	-	1	0	-
Thompson, AS	1871-73	-	-	13	2	-
Thompson, W*	1871	-	-	1	0	-
Thomson, E	1870	-	-	1	0	-

PALACE PIONEERS

Player name	Palace career	FA apps	FA goals	Total apps	Total goals	Pos.
Thornhill, F	1874	-	-	1	0	-
Tovey, A	1870	-	-	3	0	-
Trinder, OJ	1869	-	-	1	0	-
Trower, H*	1868	-	-	1	0	-
Turner, James	1862-73	1	0	44	1	G
Urwick, Frederick	1862	-	-	2	0	-
Viall, T	1873-74	1	0	6	0	H/F
Vigne, John	1871-75	3	0	31	2	B/H
Venables, G	1873	-	-	1	0	-
Walters*	1869	-	-	1	0	-
Warrington, JH	1874	1	0	1	0	-
Way, C	1874	-	-	1	0	-
Weston, C	1871	-	-	1	0	-
White, WH	1875	1	0	2	0	-
Williams, F	1874	-	-	1	0	-
Williams, V	1874-75	-	-	2	0	-
Willis, GA*	1872	-	-	1	0	-
Wilton, Francis	1873-75	1	0	7	1	G
Wood, Andrew	1862	-	-	1	0	-
Wood, Henry	1862	-	-	1	0	-
Woolley, JB	1874-75	2	0	7	0	B
Wright, J*	1867	-	-	1	0	-
Yerkins, HP*	1872	-	-	1	0	-

KEY:
* = Opposition player lent to Palace as a substitute or 'emergency'
Position: G = Goal; B = Back; H = Half back; F = Forward

Crystal Palace team line-ups

1861/62

Mar 15, 1862, Forest, A, 0-1
Allport, Bell, Cutbill, Cutbill, Day,
Head, Jackson, R Lloyd, Lloyd,
Lloyd, Medwin, Phelps, Sharland,
Turner, Urwick.

Apr 5, 1862, Forest, H, 0-4
W Allport, T Bevington, W Cutbill,
E Cutbill, Day, Jackson, T Lloyd,
H Lloyd, Lloyd, Noakes, Sharland,
Turner, Urwick, H Wood, A Wood.

1862/63

Mar 21, Forest A, 1-2

Apr 11, NN Kilburn A, 0-3
T Lloyd (c), Dry, Cutbill, Cutbill, A
Barber, Turner, F Allport, Head, W
Allport, D Allport, F Collins, Grose, W
Farquhar, Paine.

1863/64

Feb 27, Barnes A, 1-2
Turner (c), Desborough, Sharland,
Cutbill

1864/65

Nov 19, Forest, H, 0-1
D Allport, W Allport, F Collins, A
Cutbill, W Cutbill, Grose, H Lloyd,
Morris, Rhode, Sharland, Turner.

Dec 3, Barnes A, 0-0
H Lloyd, R Abraham, Irons

Dec 10, NN Kilburn A, 0-0
W Cutbill, W Allport, H Lloyd, Grose,
R Abraham, E Abraham, D Allport,
Sharland, A Cutbill, Cluff, F Collins,
Irons, Rhode, Morris, Turner.

Jan 7, Clapham Common Club, H, 0-0
Turner, R Abraham

Feb 4, Barnes H, 0-0

Feb 25, Forest A, 0-1

Mar 4, Barnes A, 2-1
Turner (c), W Allport, F Allport,
F Collins, E Cutbill, Irons, Lloyd,
Rhode, D Allport, E Abraham,
W Cutbill, Grose, H Lloyd, Morris,
Sharland.

Mar 11, Norbiton A, 5-1
Melhuish

1865/66

Oct 28, Clapham H, 2-1
Turner, R Abraham, Cockerell,
Rhode

Nov 11, Wanderers H, 1-1
Turner (c), E Abraham, W Allport,
Cockerell, W Cutbill, A Cutbill, H
Foster, Grose, T Lloyd, H Lloyd,
Lintott, Melhuish, Morten, Rhode,
Rowsell.

Nov 23, Forest School A, 1-0
E Abraham, H Lloyd

Dec 2, Barnes H, 0-0

Dec 23, Harrow Chequers, H, 1-1
Turner (c), W Allport, E Abraham,

R Abraham, A Cutbill, E Cutbill, W Cutbill, Cockerell, Dodson, H Foster, H Lloyd, T Lloyd, Morten, Tebbutt, Stephenson*.

Jan 6, Wanderers, H, 0-3
Turner (c), E Abraham, R Abraham, F Allport, W Allport, Cockerell, A Cutbill, E Cutbill, W Cutbill, H Foster, Grose, A Lloyd, H Lloyd, T Lloyd.

Mar 10, Barnes A, 0-0
Morten (c), E Abraham, D Allport, W Allport, Cockerell, A Cutbill, E Cutbill, H Foster, Grose, Hammond, A Lloyd, H Lloyd, T Lloyd, Saward, Sharland.

1866/67

Feb 9, Reigate A, 1-2
Turner, W Cutbill, A Cutbill, W Allport, Cockerell, H Lloyd, A Lloyd, H Foster, Sharland, Montresor, Wright*.

Feb 23, Reigate A, 1-0
Turner (c), W Allport, W Cutbill, E Cutbill, Cockerell, H Foster, T Lloyd, H Lloyd, A Lloyd, Morten, Montresor.

Mar 9, Forest School A, 2-2
Turner (c), W Cutbill, R Cutbill, A Cutbill, Cockerell, W Allport, D Allport, F Lloyd, A Lloyd, Carver*, Gardom*.

1867/68

Nov 30, 22 of the Club, H, 0-1
W Cutbill (c), A Cutbill, C Huggins, Cockerell, D Allport, WM Allport, H Lloyd, A Lloyd, Sharland, Butterfield, W Parr.

Dec 18, Forest School, A, 0-0
W Cutbill (c), A Cutbill, R Cutbill, D Allport, R Allport, Sharland, H Lloyd, A Lloyd, C Farquhar, Chidley, J Kolle, Ellis.

Feb 1, Reigate A, 4-0
W Cutbill (c), Turner, C Huggins, W Allport, A Lloyd, A Cutbill, R Cutbill, Butterfield, C Farquhar, W Parr.

Feb 22, Barnes A, 0-1
Turner (c), W Allport, D Allport, R Allport, Sharland, Cockerell, Chidley, W Parr, C Farquhar, A Cutbill, R Cutbill, H Daukes, H Lloyd, C Huggins.

Feb 29, Barnes A, 0-0
D Allport, Chamberlin, Cockerell, A Cutbill, R Cutbill, H Lloyd, A Lloyd, Morten, Saward, Sharland.

Mar 14, Forest School A, 1-3
A Cutbill (c), R Cutbill, Butterfield, D Allport, R Allport, W Allport, Chamberlin, H Lloyd, A Lloyd, C Huggins, B Scott, H Daukes, Saward.

Mar 21, Forest School A, 0-0
W Cutbill (c), A Cutbill, R Cutbill, D Allport, R Allport, Sharland, H Lloyd, A Lloyd, C Farquhar, J Kolle, J Ellis.

1868/69

Oct 31, Barnes A, 0-1
D Allport (c), Morten, Chamberlin, H Daukes, Stone, C Huggins, A Lloyd, Butterfield, A Cutbill, R Cutbill, G Parr, C Farquhar.

Nov 5, Mr AJ Heath's Eleven, H, 0-1
D Allport (c), WH Allport, Alpe, Barlow, A Cutbill, R Cutbill, H Daukes, Ellis, A Lintott, A Lloyd, H Lloyd.

Nov 14, Forest School, A, 0-0
D Allport (c), WM Allport, Chamberlin, A Cutbill, R Cutbill, H Daukes, C Farquhar, Harvey, C Huggins, A Lloyd, W Parr, Sharland, Stone.

Nov 28, Wanderers H, 0-1
D Allport (c), R Allport, WM Allport, A Cutbill, R Cutbill, C Farquhar, C Huggins, A Lintott, A Lloyd, T Lloyd, G Parr.

Dec 12, Clapham Common Club, A, 0-0
D Allport (c), Chamberlin, A Cutbill, R Cutbill, H Daukes, Harvey, C Huggins, T Lloyd, Morten, G Parr, Stone.

Dec 19, Reigate A, 3-1
D Allport (c), Alpe, A Cutbill, R Cutbill, Ellis, Harvey, A Lloyd, H Lloyd, T Lloyd, W Parr, Sharland, Trower*.

Jan 2, Civil Service H, 4-0
D Allport (c), F Abell, WM Allport, R Cutbill, C Farquhar, C Huggins, A Lloyd, T Lloyd, Sharland, C Smith, D Smith.

Jan 6, Mr Heath's Team, H, 2-1
D Allport (c), H Lloyd, D Smith, A Lloyd, C Smith, Sharland, R Cutbill, Morten, J Kingsford, Ellis, S Daukes.

Jan 9, Reigate, A, 1-0
D Allport (c), W Allport, Alpe, Chamberlin, R Cutbill, A Cutbill, Morten, Sharland, W Parr, Stainburn, T Lloyd.

Jan 23, Barnes, H, 0-0
D Allport (c), F Abell, Chamberlin, R Cutbill, S Daukes, Ellis, C Farquhar, A Lloyd, Morten, G Parr, C Smith.

Jan 30, Bedouins, H, 5-0
D Allport (c), F Abell, Sharland, Chamberlin, D Smith, C Smith, A Cutbill, R Cutbill, Morten, A Lintott, S Daukes.

Feb 6, West Kent, A, 1-0
D Allport (c), WM Allport, A Cutbill, Harvey, Morten, C Huggins, H Daukes, Ellis, A Lloyd, D Smith, Gower*.

Feb 20, Clapham Common Club, H, 0-1
D Allport, A Cutbill, C Farquhar, Ellis, A Lloyd, T Lloyd, F Abell, Cockerell, D Smith, R Kingsford.

Feb 24, Upton Park, A, 1-0
D Allport (c), Alpe, A Cutbill, R Cutbill, Chamberlin, WM Allport, Ellis, Harvey, C Huggins, R Kingsford, Sharland.

Feb 27, Over 23s v Under 23s, H, 4-0

Mar 6, Forest A, 2-0
D Allport (c), WM Allport, Harvey, R Kingsford, A Lloyd, T Lloyd, Sharland, T Brown*, Crowther*, Poole*, H Smith*, Walters*.

Mar 13, NN Kilburn A, 1-0
D Allport (c), WM Allport, R Cutbill, C Farquhar, Harvey, Jones, T Lloyd, G Manvell, Morten, Sharland.

Mar 27, West Kent, A, 2-0
D Allport (c), H Abell, , A Cutbill. R Cutbill, H Daukes, Chamberlin, C Farquhar, Harvey, J Kingsford, Morten, Sharland.

Apr 10, Forest A, 0-0
D Allport (c), H Abell, Alpe, Borwick, Harvey, A Lloyd, H Lloyd, Mosted, Sharland, Trinder.

1869/70

Nov 2, Forest School, A, 1-1
D Allport (c), H Abell, Borwick, A Cutbill, R Cutbill, J Kingsford, A Lloyd, Luscombe, Hartung, Slater, Stainburn.

Nov 26, Royal Engineers A, 0-1
D Allport (c), WM Allport, A Cutbill, R Cutbill, R Kingsford, Morten, G Parr, Hartung, Capper, Harvey.

Nov 30, Forest School, H, 0-0
D Allport (c), WM Allport, Borwick, W Bouch, R Cutbill, Hartung, Harvey, Luscombe, G Parr, Turner, R Solly.

Dec 4, Brixton, A, 1-0
D Allport (c), Alpe, Ellis, T Lloyd, G Manvell, E Manvell, G Parr, W Parr, E Scott, Stainburn.

Dec 4, West Kent, H, 1-1
Turner (c), H Abell, W Bouch, A Cutbill, H Daukes, C Farquhar, Harvey, C Huggins, J Kingsford, R Kingsford, A Lloyd.

Dec 11, A Morten's Ten v The Rest, H, 0-0
Morten (c), H Abell, WM Allport, A Cutbill, H Daukes, C Farquhar, Harvey, J Kingsford, A Lloyd, T Lloyd.

Dec 18, Barnes, A, 0-0
D Allport (c), H Abell, WM Allport, Clutton, Harvey, R Kingsford, A Lloyd, T Lloyd, Morten, W Parr, Turner.

Jan 5, Wanderers, H, 0-1
D Allport, C Barber, Capper, De Castro, F Kingsford, R Kingsford, A Lloyd, C Smith, C Huggins, Tovey, W Collins.

Jan 11, AJ Heath's Team, H, 2-0
D Allport (c), Abbott, Alpe, Ellis, Morten, G Parr, E Scott, H Scott, C Smith, Tovey.

Jan 26, Upton Park, A, 0-1
D Allport (c), G Parr, Harvey, Borwick, W Foster, J Kingsford, Abbott, Morten, Saxton, Hunter*

Feb 9, Wanderers, A, 2-0
D Allport (c), Abbott, Bickley, Hartung, G Parr, Body, Luscombe, Morten, Turner, H Abell.

Feb 12, Barnes, H, 0-0

Mar 5, Gipsies, A, 1-1
D Allport, WM Allport, F Abell, Abbott, H Abell, A Cutbill, C Farquhar, Heddle, Hartung, J Kingsford, R Kingsford, W Mann, Brother, G Manvell, G Parr, Moore, Soden.

Mar 12, Forest A, 0-0
A Lloyd (c), Turner, A Cutbill, C Farquhar, F Abell, H Scott, Ellis, J Kingsford, R Kingsford, Abbott, G Manvell.

Mar 12, Brixton, A, 1-0
D Allport (c), R Allport, WH Allport, WM Allport, Capper, Harvey, T Lloyd, Morten, G Parr, Tovey.

Mar 19, Forest A, 1-2
D Allport (c), Capper, Harvey, Parr, C Farquhar, R Kingsford, G Manville, Stainburn, Abbott, Turner, H Abell.

Mar 26, Upton Park, A, 0-0
D Allport (c), A Lloyd, C Huggins, G Parr, A Cutbill, Turner, Capper, Morten, WM Allport, Abbott.

1870/71

Oct 19, Upton Park, H, 3-1
D Allport (c), Borwick, Soden, Alpe, Fletcher, A Lloyd, Luscombe, Chenery, Turner, T Spreckley, C Smith.

Nov 8, Forest School, A, 1-2
Morten (c), Alcock, Chenery, Soden, A Lloyd, C Barber, Turner, T Spreckley, Hutchinson, Cazenove, Thomson.

Nov 12, Barnes, H, 0-0
D Allport (c), H Abell, R Allport, Chenery, C Farquhar, Harvey, C Huggins, R Kingsford, A Lloyd, Morris, Turner.

Nov 23, Wanderers, A, 0-2
D Allport (c), Morten, Turner, Soden, Luscombe, A Lloyd, Chenery, T Spreckley, Fletcher, H Abell, W Bouch.

Nov 26, Forest, A, 0-1
D Allport, Turner, E Scott, Alpe, Ormiston, Leete, Akenhead, G Manvell, Fletcher, C Farquhar, W Spreckley.

Dec 17, Brixton, A, 3-0
D Allport (c), WM Allport, W Cloete, Harvey, C Kolle, H Lintott, T Lloyd, G Manvell, Stainburn, Stevens.

Dec 21, Clapham Common Club, H, 1-0
D Allport (c), WM Allport, Alpe, Alcock, Baker, Harvey, Chenery, A Lloyd, Stainburn, C Smith, Fletcher.

Jan 18, Wanderers, A, 0-3
D Allport (c), WM Allport, Alpe, Chenery, C Barber, A Bouch, T Spreckley, Soden.

Jan 21, Upton Park, A, 0-1
D Allport (c), C Barber, A Bouch, C Farquhar, Heath, A Lloyd, T Lloyd, E Scott, T Spreckley, Stainburn.

Jan 21, Hampstead Heathens, H, 0-0
WM Allport, G Manvell, W Cloete, Harvey.

Feb 8, Rochester, H, 6-0
D Allport (c), Alcock, Alpe, C Barber, Fletcher, W Foster, Harvey, T Lloyd, Soden.

Feb 18, Royal Engineers, A, 1-3
D Allport (c), A Lloyd, Chenery, C Smith, Morice, T Spreckley, WM Allport, C Farquhar, Harvey, Morten, Soden.

Feb 21, Forest School, A, 1-0
D Allport (c), Alcock, WM Allport, T Lloyd, Morice, Morton, Soden, T Spreckley, Hutchinson*, Carver*, Elmslie*.

Feb 25, Captain's X v Morten's XV, H, 1-1
D Allport (c), R Allport, WM Allport, Chenery, A Cutbill, C Farquhar, Harvey, C Kolle, T Lloyd, C Smith.

Mar 4, Brixton, A, 0-0
D Allport (c), Harvey, R Allport, WM Allport, Piper, C Barber, C Smith, Ellis, T Spreckley, C Kolle, J Kolle.

Mar 18, Royal Engineers, A, 0-0
D Allport (c), R Allport, Soden, C Smith, Morice, Cockerell, Heath, Morten, Betts, Hartung, Knight.

1871/72

Oct 18, Clapham Rovers, A, 1-0
D Allport (c), Alcock, Morten, Jack, Heath, C Barber, Soden, H Abell, W Bouch, Weston.

Oct 21, Royal Engineers, H, 0-3
D Allport (c), WM Allport, Chenery, C Farquhar, Fleet, Heath, Harvey, Morten, Betts, C Smith, Soden.

Nov 4, Barnes, H, 1-0
D Allport (c), H Abell, WM Allport, W Bouch, Clutton, Cockerell, Heath, C Smith, Turner, Morice.

Nov 4, First Surrey Rifles, A, 1-0
Chenery (c), Currey, Soden, Armitage, C Kolle, C Barber, E Scott, Fleet, H Lintott, G Manvell, E Manvell, Frost*.

Nov 8, Upton Park, H, 1-0
D Allport (c), WM Allport, C Barber, Currey, Fleet, Harvey, Horne, A Lloyd, Piper, Soden, Stainburn.

Nov 11, Hitchin, A, 0-0
D Allport (c), Morten, Cockerell, Heath, W Bouch, C Smith, Soden, H Daukes, W Foster, T Spreckley, Turner.

Nov 15, Charterhouse School, A, 1-3
D Allport (c), WM Allport, L Mann, D Spreckley, C Smith, C Barber, H Daukes, Rawlinson, Highton, W Bouch, W Thompson*.

Nov 21, Forest School, A, 0-2
A Lloyd (c), Alcock, W Foster, Barber, Burrows, Highton, C Kolle, E Scott, Soden, T Spreckley, W Spreckley, Fletcher.

Nov 23, Kings School Rochester, H, 1-1
D Allport (c), WH Allport, Armitage, L Cloete, Champneys, Chenery, C Kolle, J Slaughter, Stainburn, Sharland, A Thompson.

Nov 25, Wanderers, A, 0-1
Morten (c), Currey, A Lloyd, Fleet, W Bouch, R Smith, J Smith, C Smith, Heath, Soden, H Daukes.

Nov 25, South Norwood, A, 3-0
Turner, C Farquhar, E Scott, C Barber, E Manvell, G Manvell, H Lintott, Stevens, W Foster, Piper, Saward.

Dec 16, Maidenhead, H, 3-0
D Allport (c), Heath, Morten, H Abell, WM Allport, Armitage, W Bouch, Chenery, A Lloyd, C Smith, T Spreckley.

Dec 20, Reigate, H, 2-0
Chenery (c), Currey, A Bouch, Alcock, L Neame, C Smith, A Lloyd, T Spreckley, C Barber.

Dec 23, Upton Park, A, 0-1
Morten (c), Heath, A Bouch, G Manvell, A Lloyd, T Spreckley, W Sparham, Vigne, C Barber, E Scott.

Dec 26, Harrow Chequers, H, 0-1
D Allport (c), A Bouch, W Bouch, H Abell, L Neame, R Allport, A Lloyd, Morten, Fleet, Fletcher, C Smith.

Jan 20, Wanderers, A, 0-0
D Allport (c), Heath, Rouquette, Morten, Armitage, Chenery, Chappell, Ottaway, A Lloyd, W Bouch, C Smith.

Jan 27, Charterhouse School A, 0-1
D Allport (c), WM Allport, L Neame, C Barber, Fletcher, Armitage, Vigne, Turner, A Lloyd, J Kingsford, Fleet, G Manvell.

Feb 3, Barnes, A, 2-0
D Allport (c), WM Allport, Armitage, W Bouch, C Farquhar, Fleet, C Kolle, A Lloyd, L Neame, E Scott.

Feb 3, Scoonites, A, 3-0
T Lloyd, Stainburn, R Smith

Feb 10, South Norwood A, 0-1

Feb 10, Clapham Rovers H, 3-0
D Allport (c), WM Allport, Armitage, Currey, C Farquhar, Fleet, J Kingsford, A Lloyd, Chenery, R Smith, Morten.

Feb 17, Royal Engineers, A, 0-0
D Allport, Chenery, C Farquhar, Ottaway, Morten, W Bouch, Chappell, Rouquette, L Neame, Armitage, A Lloyd.

Feb 20, Forest School, A, 1-0
Kolle

Feb 24, Captain's XI v Rest of the Club, H, 1-2
D Allport, A Bouch, A Lloyd

Mar 2, Civil Service, A, 2-1
Turner (c), T Lloyd, Fleet, WM Allport, L Neame, C Kolle, E Scott, A Bouch,

Armitage, Saward, Vigne.

Mar 9, Royal Engineers, A, 0-3
D Allport (c), WM Allport, Armitage, A Bouch, W Bouch, Chappell, Chenery, A Lloyd, Morten, Rouquette, T Spreckley.

Mar 16, South Norwood, A, 1-0
W Bouch (c), E Scott, A Bouch, Anderson, W Foster, Horne, J Kingsford, G Manvell, J Smith, R Smith, Fry.

Mar 16, Reigate Priory A, 1-0
A Lloyd, Chenery, Morten

Mar 20, First Surrey Rifles, A, 2-0
D Allport (c), Alcock, W Bouch, Chenery, Fleet, C Kolle, A Lloyd, T Lloyd, Morten, Vigne, Currey.

1872/73

Oct 12, South Norwood, A, 2-1
W Bouch (c), A Bouch, A Lloyd, Armitage, Stainburn, Cockerell, E Scott, A Thompson, R Slaughter, L Neame, Fleet, Cumberlege.

Oct 26, Oxford University, A, 2-3
Morten (c), A Bouch, Armitage, Chenery, Heath, A Lloyd, T Lloyd, Borwick, Cumberlege, Currey, Soden.

Nov 5, Forest School, H, 1-0
D Allport (c), Borwick, Brockbank, Betts, Chenery, L Neame, Stainburn, H Hutton, T Lloyd, W Spreckley, Morice.

Nov 7, Royal Engineers, 1-4

Nov 16, Barnes, A, 0-0

D Allport (c), A Bouch, W Bouch, Dorling, Fleet, J Kingsford, C Kolle, G Manvell, Soden, Turner.

Nov 23, Upton Park, H, 0-1
D Allport (c), J Kingsford, T Lloyd, C Kolle, Soden, Chenery, Cumberlege, Morten, WM Allport, R Allport, Turner.

Nov 23, Clapton Pilgrims, A, 0-1
A Bouch, T Spreckley, W Spreckley, Borwick, C Barber, Robertson, Vigne, McEwan, Masterman, Saward, Johnson.

Nov 26, Forest School, A, 0-0
D Allport (c), R Allport, Hooper, Masterman, Morice, Smouch, T Spreckley, W Spreckley, Vigne, B Powers* H Yerkins*.

Dec 7, Reigate Priory, H, 3-0
D Allport (c), WM Allport, C Barber, Chenery, W Collins, Cumberlege, Horne, C Kolle, S Hutton, G Manvell, Soden.

Dec 14, First Surrey Rifles, A, 0-1
D Allport (c), Vigne, G Manvell, E Manvell, Horne, Willis*, Greig*.

Dec 18, Wanderers, A, 2-5
D Allport (c), H Hutton, H Scott, W Spreckley, Dorling, Alpe, C Kolle, H Sparham, R Kingsford, F Kingsford, Fleet.

Dec 26, Harrow Chequers, H, 3-0
D Allport (c), A Bouch, C Bouch, W Bouch, Cumberlege, Dorling, Fleet, Morten, A Lloyd, H Sparham, Turner.

Dec 28, Windsor Home Park, H, 0-1
D Allport (c), A Bouch, W Bouch, A Lloyd, T Lloyd, Morten, H Sparham, Stainburn, W Foster, Fleet, Vigne.

Jan 4, Clapham Rovers, A, 0-1
A Bouch (c), E Scott, Vigne, J Kingsford, F Kingsford, W Spreckley, Horne, McEwan, L Hutton, C Barber, H Sparham.

Jan 4, South Norwood, H, 3-2
D Allport (c), WM Allport, Armitage, W Collins, Fleet, T Lloyd, C Kolle, Heath, Stainburn, A Thompson.

Jan 11, Clapton Pilgrims, H, 4-0
D Allport (c), WM Allport, Fleet, S Hutton, T Lloyd, Saward, Stainburn, A Thompson, Vigne.

Jan 18, Barnes, H, 2-0
D Allport (c), WM Allport, Armitage, W Collins, Cumberlege, Chenery, Fleet, A Lloyd, A Thompson, Turner, Vigne.

Jan 25, Upton Park, A, 3-2
Morten (c), Armitage, Borwick, A Bouch, W Bouch, W Collins, Fry, A Lloyd, Soden, H Sparham.

Jan 25, Leyton, H, 9-2
D Allport (c), C Barber, J Kingsford, C Kolle, S Hutton, T Lloyd, Saward, A Thompson, Vigne, Fleet/Champneys.

Feb 8, Reigate Priory, A, 1-1
D Allport (c), WM Allport, H Cloete, Cumberlege, Fleet, C Kolle, S Hutton, J Kingsford, D Parbury, A Thompson, Vigne.

Feb 22, Clapham Rovers, H, 1-2
D Allport (c), S Hutton, L Cloete, Turner, Dorling, A Lloyd, T Lloyd, Horne, J Kingsford, Cumberlege, Chenery.

Feb 22, First Surrey Rifles, A, 0-1
Morten (c), Masterman, A Bouch, Armitage, Vigne, C Bouch, Fleet, A Thompson, WM Allport, S Parbury, C Kolle.

Mar 15, Clapham Rovers, A, 0-3
A Lloyd (c), Armitage, C Barber, H Cloete, Dorling, WM Allport, Fleet, S Hutton, G Manvell, D Parbury, Looking.

Mar 22, Royal Engineers, A, 0-3
Morten (c), Bonsor, Cumberlege, Armitage, H Cloete, W Cloete, W Bouch, Heath, C Kolle, Venables, L Hutton.

1873/74

Oct 11, South Norwood, H, 3-2
L Neame (c), Turner, E Scott, T Lloyd, C Barber, Chenery, Dorling, Soden, E Manvell, Morten.

Oct 11, Barnes, A, 0-1
D Allport (c), L Cloete, A Cloete, Fleet, G Neame, Armitage, A Thompson, F Abraham, C Kolle, Viall, Masterman.

Oct 18, Swifts, A, 0-1
L Neame (c), F Abraham, Fleet, Currey, Masterman, Armitage, W Bouch, Soden, L Cloete, Dorling, D Allport.

Oct 25, Woodford Wells, H, 1-2
L Neame (c), G Neame, T Lloyd, Horne, Dorling, Milverton, Currey, E Manvell, Cumberlege, W Bouch, C Bouch.

Oct 25, Reigate Priory, A, 0-2
D Allport (c), Masterman, L Cloete,

Alpe, Wilton, A Thompson, Fleet, Turner, B Richardson*, Craig*.

Nov 5, Upton Park, H, 2-2
D Allport (c), R Allport, Fraser, E Manvell, W Maynard, Morice, G Neame, L Neame, W Spreckley, Viall.

Nov 8, Royal Engineers, H, 1-3
R Kingsford (c), Turner, Masterman, L Cloete, Chenery, Heron, Clutton, Cumberlege, Currey, W Bouch, L Neame.

Nov 11, Forest School, H, 1-0
D Allport (c), R Allport, L Neame, Chenery, Viall, S Parbury, Oelrichs, W Maynard, Hooper, G Neame, Cumberlege.

Nov 22, Clapham Rovers, H, 0-3
L Neame (c), Currey, Masterman, G Neame, Cumberlege, Wilton, Fleet, Milverton, Oelrichs, Smithies.

Nov 22, Brondesbury, A, 1-3
Morten, H Cloete, A Cloete, C Barber, R Abraham, N Abraham, Burt, S Brown, Rutley, Goodfellow*

Dec 3, Charterhouse School A, 0-2
D Allport (c), F Maynard, Masterman, EH Bambridge, Cumberlege, Alpe, A Thompson, Soden, R Allport, T Spreckley.

Dec 6, Maidenhead, H, 1-3
D Allport (c), W Cloete, Currey, Fleet, C Smith, Armitage, A Thompson, Cumberlege, Horne, G Neame, S Parbury.

Dec 6, Leyton, A, 5-0
L Neame (c), Turner, Masterman, EH Bambridge, Dorling, Smithies, Wilton,

G Manvell, Hubbard, C Bouch.

Dec 9, Forest School, A, 0-0
D Allport (c), R Allport, Fraser,
Masterman, W Maynard,
L Neame, S Parbury, H Smith,
W Spreckley, Vigne.

Dec 17, Gitanos, H, 3-0
D Allport, R Allport, Chenery, Alpe,
Alcock, Soden, Cumberlege, W
Maynard, Fleet, C Smith, Currey.

Dec 20, Barnes, H, 4-0
L Neame (c), Currey, Masterman,
Alcock, R Kingsford, Chenery,
Cumberlege, C Smith, Oelrichs,
Milverton, A Thompson.

Dec 20, Pilgrims, A, 0-4
D Allport (c), Alpe, Armitage, Vigne,
Dorling, G Neame, Fleet, H Cloete,
Champneys.

Dec 26, South Norwood, H, 5-1
D Allport, Oelrichs, Currey, Milverton,
Vigne, L Neame, C Smith, R
Kingsford, F Kingsford, Fleet,
Chenery.

Dec 27, Reigate Priory, H, 3-2
D Allport (c), Masterman, Fleet,
Soden, Oelrichs, Cumberlege,
F Kingsford, C Smith, L Neame,
Champneys, Chenery.

Jan 3, First Surrey Rifles, H, 1-1
L Neame (c), D Allport, Soden,
Fleet, Cumberlege, Vigne, Alpe,
Champneys, Ford, C Smith.

Jan 17, First Surrey Rifles, A, 0-1
L Neame (c), Currey, Masterman,
Ford, V Williams, C Smith, Fleet,
Smithies, S Parbury.

Jan 21, Pilgrims, A, 1-0
L Neame (c), Masterman, G Manvell,
F Maynard, W Maynard, Hooper, R
Allport, W Foster, Romilly, C Smith,
Wilton.

Jan 24, Clapham Rovers, A, 0-3

Jan 24, Brondesbury, H, 2-3
Morten, Ford, Fleet, W Spreckley,
Stephens, Vigne, Horne, Dorling,
Smithies, S Parbury.

Jan 28, Rochester, H, 3-2
Chenery, Kingsford

Feb 16, Nottingham, H, 1-1
C Smith (c), Chenery, D Allport,
Fleet, R Kingsford, Cumberlege,
Viall, F Williams, R Allport, H
Bevington, Heron.

Mar 7, Gitanos, A, 0-1
L Neame, Masterman, J Kingsford, J
Brown, Fleet, Cumberlege, C Smith,
Alpe, Fraser, H Bevington, Ford.

Mar 14, Maidenhead, A, 0-1
L Neame (c), R Kingsford, J
Kingsford, S Parbury, C Smith, Fleet,
Brockbank, G Neame, Masterman, C
Brown.

Mar 21, Royal Engineers, A, 0-2
R Kingsford (c), Birley, J Kingsford,
Masterman, Chenery, Heron,
Cumberlege, C Smith, Armitage,
Brockbank, EH Bambridge.

Mar 28, Upton Park, 0-3

1874/75

Oct 24, Clapham Rovers, A, 1-1
Savage, D Smith

Oct 29, Swifts, A, 0-1
C Smith (c), Soden, L Neame, D Allport, T Spreckley, W Spreckley, W Bouch, W Maynard, Masterman, Fleet, Savage.

Oct 31, Upton Park, A, 0-2
Wilton, C Smith, D Smith, L Neame, Armitage, A Lloyd, Savage, Keen, Vigne, Soden, C Barber.

Nov 3, Forest School, A, 1-4
C Smith, L Neame, F Maynard, D Allport, T Spreckley, W Spreckley, W Maynard, D Smith, R Allport, Fleet, A Lloyd.

Nov 7, Gitanos, H, 2-0
C Smith (c), Chenery, L Neame, E Barlow, F Barlow, Armitage, Fleet, D Smith, Viall, Savage, Ford.

Nov 14, Cambridge University, A, 0-0
C Smith (c), Alpe, E Barlow, F Barlow, Currey, Morten, L Neame, Savage, Viall, Warrington, Woolley.

Nov 14, South Norwood, H, 3-0
Chenery, Philpott, Fleet, Ford, Cumberlege, Bouch, Lloyd, Masterman, Boosey, Smith, Richardson, Vigne.

Nov 18, Westminster School, A, 1-3
C Smith (c), L Neame, Fleet, Borman, Thornhill, Elmslie, Morten, Brewer, Vigne, W Foster, Long-staffe*.

Nov 21, Cambridge University, H, 1-2
C Smith (c), Armitage, E Barlow, F Barlow, Currey, Fleet, A Lloyd, Morten, L Neame, Savage, Woolley.

Dec 9, Upton Park, H, 0-3
C Smith (c), F Barlow, Way, R Allport, WM Allport, Foster, Keen, Morice, A Lloyd, Frank, Romilly.

Dec 12, Royal Engineers, H, 1-2
C Smith (c), Chenery, R Kingsford, F Barlow, Birley, Ford, Morice, Masterman, Savage.

Jan 9, Reigate Priory, H, 5-0
C Smith (c), L Neame, G Neame, Savage, Fox, Barry, S le B Smith, H le B Smith, W Allport, Woolley, D Smith.

Jan 23, First Surrey Rifles, A, 0-2
C Smith (c), Vigne, EH Bambridge, Chenery, Horne, Woolley, Simpson, GF Bambridge.

Feb 6, Brondesbury Park, A, 3-0
C Smith (c), Chenery, L Neame, Maddison, Buchanan, Morice, D Smith, H Solly, Woolley, Vigne, Savage.

Feb 11, Westminster School, A, 5-0
C Smith (c), R Kingsford, L Neame, Chenery, Maddison, Buchanan, Savage, C Barber, Alcock, R Allport, Lindsay, W Foster.

Feb 13, Barnes, A, 0-3
C Smith (c), L Neame, Vigne, A Boosey, W Cloete, EH Bambridge, Woolley, D Smith.

Feb 27, Pilgrims, A, 0-2
C Smith (c), Savage, W Bouch, J Kingsford, L Neame, EH Bambridge, Philpott, D Smith, Woolley, Keen, F Barlow.

Mar 6, Leyton, A, 7-1

Mar 9, Forest School, A, 2-4

1875/76

Oct 23, Clapham Rovers, A, 1-4
C Smith (c), Armitage, L Neame, G Neame, Field, G Boosey, C Barber, Ferguson, W Cloete.

Oct 30, Woodford Wells, A, 0-0
C Smith (c), D Smith, L Neame, Armitage, W Huggins, Burls, Ferguson, Vigne, Pittis, Wilton.

Nov 6, 105th Regiment, A, 0-0
C Smith (c), W Bouch, Vigne, W Cloete, Wilton, E Barlow, F Barlow, L Neame, Dorling, Armitage, White.

Nov 13, First Surrey Rifles, A, 0-0
C Smith, W Cloete, Vigne, F Barlow, L Neame, D Smith, Ferguson, E Barlow, Morice, A Huggins, Armitage.

Nov 17, Westminster School, A, 2-2
C Smith (c), W Cloete, Vigne, Ford, Savage, D Allport, D Smith, White, F Barlow, L Neame, V Williams.

Nov 20, 105th Regiment, A 3-0
C Smith (c), W Bouch, L Neame, D Smith, E Barlow, F Barlow, Vigne, Savage, W Cloete, Ford, Armitage, Dorling.

Nov 27, Forest School, A, 0-4

Dec 11, Wanderers, A, 0-3
C Smith (c), Savage, D Smith, E Barlow, Vigne, Armitage, Dorling, W Bouch, Ferguson, W Cloete.

Dec 18, Barnes, A, 0-3
C Smith (c), L Neame, F Barlow, D Smith, Armitage, H Abell, Hubbard, Sedgwick, W Cloete, D Allport, Ferguson.

KEY:
* = Opposition player lent to Palace as a substitute or 'emergency'
(c) = Captain

Crystal Palace timeline

1861 – A Crystal Palace football team is formed by members of the Crystal Palace Cricket Club.

1862 – The footballers play their first game against Forest FC in March. Their home fixtures take place on a portion of the cricket ground.

1863 – Officials from Crystal Palace help found the Football Association with 10 other clubs and they agree on the first set of laws for the game.

1864 – CPFC host their matches in Billet Field, in Penge. Their February clash with Barnes is only the second ever FA-sanctioned football match.

1867 – Palace make a return to Crystal Palace Park for their home venue.

1871 – They are the original participants of the FA Cup, which is football's first knockout cup competition and reach the semi-final. Palace captain Douglas Allport helps source the original trophy.

1872 – Palace forward Charles Chenery is selected for the world's first-ever football international, Scotland v England.

1875 – CPFC play their last recorded game against Barnes in December.

1876 – The club disbands with no further matches reported in the press. It is no longer affiliated with the FA. The Crystal Palace cricket side continues with its fixtures.

1883 – A team calling itself Crystal Palace Rovers plays one reported game against the Pilgrims.

1895 – The Crystal Palace Company builds a sports arena in the park and begins staging the FA Cup Finals. The company creates a new team made up of Corinthian FC players which entertains Aston Villa.

1896 – Another Palace line-up is assembled and it takes on the German FA.

1897 – The Crystal Palace holds its first England international at the stadium. Palace play another exhibition match against Sheffield Wednesday.

1905 – Crystal Palace Football & Athletic Club Ltd is formed, with the Crystal Palace Company the majority shareholder. The new professional outfit joins Division Two of the Southern League.

Crystal Palace sports arena

FA Cup Finals at Crystal Palace

1895	Aston Villa	1-0	West Brom	42,560
1896	The Wednesday	2-1	Wolves	48,836
1897	Aston Villa	3-2	Everton	65,891
1898	Nottingham Forest	3-1	Derby County	62,017
1899	Sheffield Utd	4-1	Derby County	73,833
1900	Bury	4-0	Southampton	68,945
1901	Tottenham	2-2	Sheffield Utd	110,820
1902	Sheffield Utd	1-1	Southampton	76,914
1902	(R) Sheffield Utd	2-1	Southampton	33,068
1903	Bury	6-0	Derby County	63,102
1904	Manchester City	1-0	Bolton	61,374
1905	Aston Villa	2-0	Newcastle Utd	101,117
1906	Everton	1-0	Newcastle Utd	75,609
1907	The Wednesday	2-1	Everton	84,594
1908	Wolves	3-1	Newcastle Utd	74,697
1909	Manchester Utd	1-0	Bristol City	71,401
1910	Newcastle Utd	1-1	Barnsley	77,747
1911	Bradford City	0-0	Newcastle Utd	69,068
1912	Barnsley	0-0	West Brom	54,556
1913	Aston Villa	1-0	Sunderland	120,081
1914	Burnley	1-0	Liverpool	72,778

Highest FA Cup Final attendances

1. Bolton 2-0 West Ham (1923), Wembley Stadium – 126,047
2. Aston Villa 1-0 Sunderland (1913), Crystal Palace – 120,081
3. Tottenham 2-2 Sheffield Utd (1901), Crystal Palace – 110,820
4. Aston Villa 2-0 Newcastle Utd (1905), Crystal Palace – 101,117

England internationals at Crystal Palace

April 3, 1897, England 1-2 Scotland – 33,715
March 30, 1901, England 2-2 Scotland – 18,250
April 1, 1905, England 1-0 Scotland – 27,599
April 3, 1909, England 2-0 Scotland – 23,667

Teams that played at Crystal Palace

Corinthians: 1897-05 and 1922-37
Crystal Palace: 1905-15
Casuals: 1922-25

Timeline of major world events

1861 – Abraham Lincoln is sworn in as president of the United States (March). The American Civil War begins (April). Queen Victoria's husband, Prince Albert, dies from typhoid, aged 42 (December).

1863 – The world's first underground railway opens in London, with Paddington to Farringdon Street the inaugural section (January).

1864 – Gerard Adriaan Heineken, aged 22, takes over the Haystack brewery in Amsterdam, deciding to brew only lager (February).

1865 – President Lincoln dies from a gunshot wound, aged 56. The Civil War ends (both April). The first speed limit is introduced in Britain: 2mph in towns and 4mph in the country (July). John Russell is UK prime minister for the second time (October).

1866 – Edward Smith-Stanley is named prime minister for a third time (June).

1867 – British surgeon Joseph Lister publishes his discovery of disinfectant (March).

1868 – Benjamin Disraeli is UK prime minister for the first time (February). The last British public execution is carried out (May). William Gladstone is named UK prime minister. The world's first traffic lights are installed in London (both December).

1869 – Sainsbury's first store, in Drury Lane, London, is unveiled (May). The Suez Canal opens, linking the Mediterranean and the Red Sea (November).

1870 – The Elementary Education Act means compulsory education in England and Wales for children aged between five and 13 (August).

1871 – Englishman Charles Babbage, who created the modern computer, dies aged 79 (October).

1873 – Levi Strauss and Jacob Davis receive a US patent for blue jeans, with copper rivets (May).

1874 – Benjamin Disraeli is installed as prime minister (February).

1876 – Scotsman Alexander Graham Bell receives a patent for revolutionary new invention, the telephone (March). Queen Victoria is declared empress of India (May). Heinz Tomato Ketchup is created in Pittsburgh, USA (June).

Bibliography

BOOKS
CPFC 1861 or 1905? – Mark Metcalf and Clive Nicholson
Cricket at the Crystal Palace, WG Grace and the London County Cricket Club –
Brian Pearce
England Players' Records: 1872 - 2020 – Graham Betts
Football Annuals 1868-1881 – Charles Alcock
Football: Our Winter Game – Charles W Alcock
Lost Teams of the South – Mike Bradbury
Palace at the Palace: A History of the Crystal Palace and its Football Club 1851-1915
– Peter Manning
People of the Palace, The Crystal Palace Company & Trust – JP Craddock
Rutland Barrington, a Record of Thirty-Five Years' Experience On the English Stage
– Rutland Barrington
The Book of Rules of the Game of Foot-ball – Charles W Alcock
The Father of Modern Sport: The Life and Times of Charles W Alcock – Keith Booth
The First Crystal Palace Football Club 1861-1876 – Stuart Hibberd
The Football Association 1863-1883: A Source Book – Tony Brown
The Forest Club (Leytonstone) – David Ian Chapman
The Origin of Crystal Palace FC, Vol 1 – Steve Martyniuk
The Wanderers FC, Five Times FA Cup Winners – Rob Cavallini
The Wow Factor, A Concise History of Early Soccer and the Men Who Made It –
John Blythe Smart
To the Palace for the Cup – Ian Bevan, Stuart Hibberd and Michael Gilbert

NEWSPAPERS AND PERIODICALS
The Aberdeen Journal
The Advertiser
The Athletic News
Bell's Life in London and Sporting Chronicle
Cricket: A weekly record of the game
The Carthusian magazine of Charterhouse
The Daily News
The Elizabethan magazine of Westminster School
The El Paso Times
Forest School Magazine
The Globe
The Graphic
The Illustrated Police News
The London Evening Standard

The Morning Post
The Morning Advertiser
The Norwood News
The Norwood News & Crystal Palace Chronicle
The Nottinghamshire Guardian
Penny Illustrated Paper
The Scotsman
The Sheffield Daily Telegraph
The Sheffield and Rotherham Independent
The South London Chronicle
The Sporting Gazette
The Sportsman
The Sporting Life
The Sporting Times
The Sunderland Daily Echo
The Surrey Comet
The Sussex Agricultural Express
The Sydney Mail
The Sydney Morning Herald

WEBSITES

Ancestry.co.uk
Britishnewspaperarchive.co.uk
Englandfootballonline.com
Espncricinfo.com
Historicalkits.co.uk
Holmesdale.net
Newspapers.com
Rmslusitania.info
Scottishsporthistory.com
Wikipedia.com

PHOTO CREDITS

P8 – Dickinsons' comprehensive pictures of the Great Exhibition of 1851;
Philip Henry Delamotte (1821–1889) - Smithsonian Libraries
P10 – J. McNeven - collections.vam.ac.uk
P11 – CC-by-sa2.0, jes from Melbourne, Australia - don't chop the dinosaurs daddy
P14 – S.T. Dadd - Scanned from the book Historia del Futbol
P18 – The London News
P27 – John Nixon
P32 – Adrian Roebuck
P34 – Pubwiki.co.uk
P39 – Whatpub.com

Printed in Great Britain
by Amazon

18274598R00120